Regional Economic Integration in the Middle East and North Africa

Regional Economic Integration in the Middle East and North Africa

Beyond Trade Reform

Mustapha Rouis
Steven R. Tabor

THE WORLD BANK
Washington, D.C.

ISBN (paper): 978-0-8213-9726-8
ISBN (electronic): 978-0-8213-9729-9
DOI: 10.1596/978-0-8213-9726-8

Cover illustration: Malika Drissi; *Cover design:* Naylor Design

Library of Congress Cataloging-in-Publication Data
Rouis, Mustapha.
Regional economic integration in the Middle East and North Africa : beyond trade reform/Mustapha Rouis and Steven R. Tabor.
  p. cm. — (Directions in development)
  Includes bibliographical references.
  ISBN 978-0-8213-9726-8 (alk. paper) — ISBN 978-0-8213-9729-9
1. Middle East—Commercial policy. 2. Africa, North—Commercial policy. 3. Middle East—Foreign economic relations. 4. Africa, North—Foreign economic relations. 5. Middle East—Economic integration. 6. Africa, North—Economic integration. I. Tabor, Steven R. II. World Bank. III. Title.
  HF1583.3.R68 2012
  337.1'56—dc23
                                                                                2012035603

Contents

Boxes

Figures

Tables

Preface

Economic integration—globally and regionally—could make an important contribution to growth, employment generation, and poverty reduction in the Middle East and North Africa (MENA) region. This report summarizes what is known about the constraints to and opportunities for deepening economic integration within the MENA region and beyond. It discusses aspects of economic integration that are often neglected in economic analyses of the topic, especially physical connectivity, cross-border trade facilitation, infrastructure network development, and the vital role of logistics services.

There is a clear and compelling case for MENA countries to deepen and expand reforms to enhance economic integration so as to become more competitive. The focus in MENA must be on opening up to the rest of the world, including countries within the region. Regional and global integration policies must be designed to complement one another in order to avoid costly diversion of trade and misallocation of resources. Deepening economic integration will require action on many fronts—from trade and investment policies to critical investments in improving border facilitation institutions and seamlessly integrating economic infrastructure throughout the region. Measures designed to foster regional economic integration often have the added benefit of bolstering competitiveness and productivity across the economy, bringing down costs to consumers, and boosting job creation in industries whose markets are steadily expanding.

This report is part of a broader World Bank initiative to place trade and economic integration at center stage in promoting stronger economic performance in the Arab world. It serves as a companion report to *From Political to Economic Awakening in the Arab World: The Path of Economic Integration*, a study on trade and foreign direct investment prepared for the Deauville Partnership by the World Bank, at the request of the G8 and in coordination with the Islamic Development Bank and the Marseille Center for Mediterranean Integration. The Deauville report addresses the five so-called Partnership countries—the Arab Republic of Egypt, Jordan, Libya, Morocco, and Tunisia, which are undergoing fundamental political and economic transition—and identifies priority areas in helping to integrate these countries into the global economy through enhanced trade and foreign direct investment. The study that follows here covers a broader set of MENA countries and provides more in-depth background information and analysis on the priority reform areas.

Taken together, these two reports offer a simple but powerful message to the leaders of the Arab world. Economic integration, both regionally and globally, is key to spurring the growth and employment creation so urgently needed to increase the well-being of the population and consolidate ongoing political transitions in the MENA region.

Inger Andersen
Vice President
Middle East and North Africa Region
World Bank

Acknowledgments

This report was prepared by a World Bank team consisting of Mustapha Rouis (principal author); Steven R. Tabor (co-author); Jean-Pierre Chauffour (trade policy and preferential trade agreements); Ndiame Diop (trade in services); Graham Smith (transport sector); Husam M. Beides (power sector); Kaoru Kimura, Victor Mulas, Carlo Maria Rossotto, and Junko Narimatsu (information and communication technology); Jean Francois Arvis, Ben Shepherd, and Abdemoula Ghzala (cross-border trade facilitation); Caroline L. Freund and Luis Alberto Portugal (gravity model); and Michael Stanton-Geddes (data analysis). Isabelle Chaal-Dabi provided valuable administrative assistance, and Amanda Green and Carolyn Goldinger edited the report. The report was prepared under the guidance of Caroline L. Freund (Chief Economist, Middle East and North Africa Region, World Bank). Designated reviewers were Bernard Hoekman and Farrukh Iqbal from the World Bank and Jamel Eddine Zarrouk from the Arab Monetary Fund, all of whom provided valuable comments. Helpful comments and inputs were also provided by Jean-Pierre Chauffour, Manuela V. Ferro, Hiau Looi Kee, Lili Mottaghi, Mariam J. Sherman, Jonathan D. Walters, and Christina A. Wood, all World Bank staff.

About the Authors

Mustapha Rouis is Lead Economist in the Chief Economist's Office of the World Bank's Middle East and North Africa Region. During his long tenure at the World Bank, he has worked on East Asia, Africa, Europe and Central Asia, Latin America and the Caribbean, and the Middle East and North Africa. He served as Country Manager for Yemen and Tajikistan. His work has covered a variety of economic topics, including policy reform, public sector management, trade policy, and development assistance.

Steven R. Tabor is an economist and director of an economics advisory firm in the Netherlands. He has worked as an advisor to governments in Asia, Africa, Europe, Latin America, and the Pacific. He has provided assistance to several multilateral development banks in development evaluation, strategy formulation, and quality assurance. His work has centered on public finance, development planning, regional integration, monitoring and evaluation, poverty reduction, and aid effectiveness.

Abbreviations

AfDB	African Development Bank
AICTO	Arab Information and Communications Technology Organization
AMU	Arab Maghreb Union
ARAGNET	Arab Regulators Network
ASEAN	Association of Southeast Asian Nations
ASYCUDA	Automated System for Customs Data
CBTFI	Cross-Border Trade Facilitation and Infrastructure Plan
CETMO	Centre for Transportation Studies for the Western Mediterranean
COMESA	Common Market for Eastern and Southern Africa
EIB	European Investment Bank
ECI	Eight-Country and Territories Interconnection (Arab Republic of Egypt, Iraq, Jordan, Lebanon, Libya, Syrian Arab Republic, and Turkey) and West Bank and Gaza
EFTA	European Free Trade Association
EU	European Union
FDI	Foreign direct investment
FRATEL	Réseau Francophone de la Régulation des Télecommunications
FTA	Free Trade Agreement

GAFTA	Greater Arab Free Trade Agreement
GATS	General Agreement on Trade in Services
GATT	General Agreement on Tariffs and Trade
GCC	Gulf Cooperation Council
GDP	Gross domestic product
GPS	Global positioning system
GTMO	Transport Group of the Western Mediterranean
ICT	Information and communications technology
IPR	Intellectual property rights
IRU	International Road Transport Union
IsDB	Islamic Development Bank
IT-BPO	Information technology and business process outsourcing
LPI	Logistics Performance Index
LSCI	Liner Shipping Connectivity Index
MENA	Middle East and North Africa
MERCOSUR	Mercado Comun del Sur (Southern Common Market)
MFN	Most favored nation
NAFTA	North American Free Trade Agreement
NAMA	Nonagricultural market access
NTMs	Nontariff measures
OTRI	Overall Trade Restrictiveness Index
OTRI_T	Tariff-only Overall Trade Restrictiveness Index
PAAP	Program of Support for Professional Associations
PAFTA	Pan Arab Free Trade Agreement
PAIGAM	Program to provide guarantees
QIZ	Qualifying industrial zone
PTA	Preferential Trade Agreement
REM	Regional Electricity Market
SPS	Sanitary and phytosanitary
STRI	Services Trade Restrictiveness Indices
TBT	Technical barriers to trade
TEU	Twenty-foot Equivalent Unit
TIR	Transports Internationaux Routiers (International Road Transport)
TNO	Transnational operators
TSO	Transmission system operator
TRIPS	Trade-related aspects of intellectual property rights
UNCTAD	United Nations Conference on Trade and Development
USAID	United States Agency for International Development
WBG	West Bank and Gaza
WCO	World Customs Organization
WTO	World Trade Organization

Overview

Limited integration has stifled the Middle East and North Africa (MENA) region's ability to tap into its significant potential for economic growth and job creation. The MENA region is among the least integrated in the world economy. Although home to 5.5 percent of the world's population (on average for 2008–10) and 3.9 percent of the world's gross domestic product (GDP), the region's share of nonoil world trade is only 1.8 percent. By contrast, countries that have opted for a liberal trade and investment regime—most notably in East Asia—have experienced a significant increase in trade, employment, and per capita income. If petroleum and gas are taken into consideration, the MENA region is far more integrated in the world economy, with total exports accounting for 6.2 percent of total world trade. Exports of oil and gas represent about three-quarters of MENA's total exports.

This study shows that, in spite of commendable reform efforts in recent years, the MENA region continues to face constraints to economic competitiveness in general, and trade barriers in particular. Of critical importance is the need to improve trade-related infrastructure and strengthen trade facilitation activities. Moreover, this study demonstrates that preferential trade agreements (PTAs), though helpful in many respects, do not significantly expand exports. Instead, the focus in MENA must be on opening up to the rest of the world, which may require that individual countries aggressively pursue unilateral liberalization policies. While regional cooperation and integration can bring benefits, these efforts can also pose significant costs if not carried out in a manner that is compatible with broader global integration trends. Finally, while there is reasonable potential to enhance trade in goods, trade in services is a major untapped source of trade growth within the region and between the region and the rest of the world.

Why Integrate?

Deep economic integration could help policy makers address the critical development challenges that have been brought to the forefront by the Arab Spring. The MENA region faces a number of serious economic management challenges, including high youth unemployment, global commodity market shocks, weak governance, and inefficient public sectors. The Arab Spring has unleashed a torrent of protests across the region, giving voice to popular frustrations with exclusive, ineffective, and inefficient policy choices. This movement has brought to the forefront the need for policy makers to refocus their development strategies on inclusive growth, job creation, and good governance. The region's leaders are sensitive to the calls for reform and are accelerating measures to stimulate job growth, make the economic growth process more inclusive, and foster popular participation in the development process.

Economic cooperation and integration could help address these challenges by boosting growth, fostering diversification, and stimulating employment. In particular, trade and foreign direct investment (FDI) matter for generating the jobs that the region so badly requires. Regional cooperation can make a difference in attracting the investment needed to generate more and better jobs by removing barriers to capital inflows and by creating a better enabling environment for both domestic and foreign investment.

Regional cooperation and global economic integration are complementary processes. Regional integration contributes to global integration by reaping the benefits of geographical proximity, promoting learning by doing, and fostering efforts to build competitiveness. Global integration can place added pressure on countries to improve integration within their region. In many respects, regional cooperation and integration can be understood as a stepping-stone to wider global market cooperation, with regional infrastructure investment and trade in goods, services, and factors within the region serving to boost competitiveness and encourage the development of the institutions necessary for integration on a wider scale.

Tapping Significant Trade Potential

It is well established that the MENA region has performed far below its economic potential over the past three decades. Despite large resource endowments, the region's per capita income grew by only 0.9 percent per year, on average, over the past three decades. This modest growth compares unfavorably with all other regions except Sub-Saharan Africa. While growth in per capita income picked up over the past decade to average 2.2 percent annually, and while the pace of job creation, measured in terms of employment-growth elasticity, increased faster than in other parts of the world, unemployment has remained high. It is estimated that the region created only 3.2 million jobs per year over the past decade—less than half of the number of jobs needed. Simulation analysis suggests that average annual per capita economic growth will have to nearly double over the next decades (to about 4 percent) in order for MENA to address its employment deficit. Performance in the region is hampered by a narrow economic base, low productivity, and lack of integration in the world economy, as reflected in its modest nonoil trade share.

The MENA region as a whole is characterized by exports of primary commodities, largely oil and gas (76 percent in 2008–10). Manufactured goods account for just over 11 percent of exports, and other sectors account for the remaining 13 percent. MENA countries' exports are highly concentrated and less diversified overall, with the Arab Republic of Egypt, Jordan, Lebanon, Morocco, and Tunisia faring better than the rest of the region on both indicators. While most countries have made some improvements in export diversification over the past 15 years, the level of diversification remains quite low compared to the world average. Furthermore, exports are generally produced with low levels of skill and could be classified as unsophisticated. For example, only 21 percent of total exports from the above five countries are classified as medium- or high-technology, compared with almost 37 percent of exports in other middle-income economies. This combination of limited export diversification and low-technology industry hampers productivity growth in MENA, which is already low given the countries' income levels.

Despite improvements, MENA is one of the least globally and regionally integrated regions in the world. The region's share in total world
exports of nonoil goods remained below 1 percent for a long time, gradually increasing during the past decade to reach 1.8 percent in 2008–10
(figure O.1). Similarly, despite doubling its services exports, MENA's
share in total services trade has stagnated at between 2 and 3 percent
during the past two decades. Most MENA countries have begun to open
up their economies in the past decade. The United Arab Emirates, Qatar,
Kuwait, Egypt, Jordan, Oman, and the Islamic Republic of Iran have wit-
nessed the most rapid growth in exports within the region. Among the oil
importers, Egypt and Jordan have made significant progress in diversify-
ing exports. Likewise, most Gulf Cooperation Council (GCC) exports
have reflected a reduced dependence on crude exports in favor of processed industrial goods, including chemicals, fertilizers, and other processed petroleum products.

Though on a rising trend, integration within the MENA region has
remained low, particularly in comparison to other middle- and high-
income regions. Intraregional exports of goods have averaged less than
8 percent of total exports in the MENA region over the 2008–10 period,
as compared to 25 percent in the Association of Southeast Asian Nations
(ASEAN) and 66 percent in the European Union (EU) (figure O.2). The
countries that trade the most within MENA are oil importers, particularly

Figure O.1   MENA's Export Share in the World of Nonfuel Goods and Services

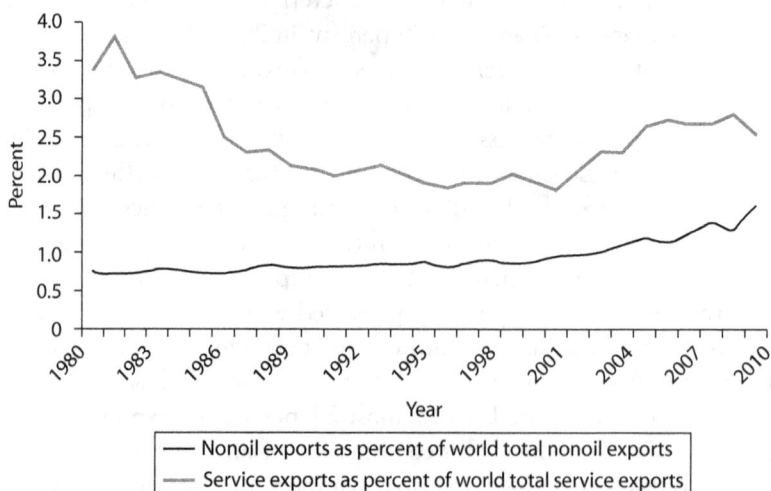

Sources: World Integrated Trade Solution (WITS) database and World Development Indicators (2012).

Figure O.2   Share of Exports within Regions

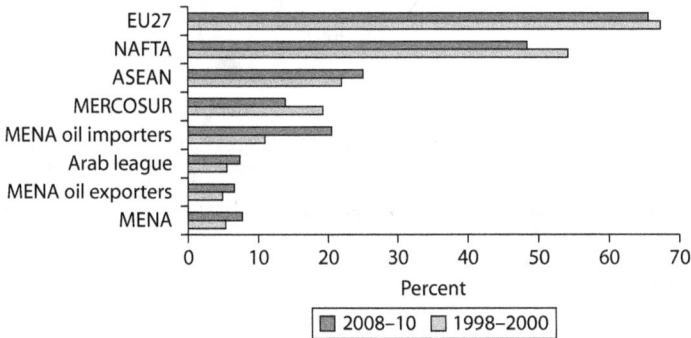

Source: Table C.13.

those Mashreq countries with strong links to the GCC (45 percent of their exports are within MENA) and Egypt (28 percent). Maghreb countries, which have close ties with the EU, export the least within the MENA region (less than 5 percent) and among themselves.

Significant progress has been made in reducing barriers to trade in goods within the MENA region and, to some extent, between the region and the rest of the world. Over the last decade, preferential liberalization under the Pan Arab Free Trade Area (PAFTA) and other PTAs has been complemented by reductions in most favored nation (MFN) tariffs. As a result, the average uniform tariff equivalent of all tariffs (ad valorem and specific) for the region fell from nearly 15 percent in 2002 to 6 percent in 2009. In fact, MENA was the region in which tariffs decreased the most during the global financial crisis, especially on manufacturing goods.

Notwithstanding progress made in the last decade, the level of tariff protection in the MENA region vis-à-vis the rest of the world remains high by international standards. According to the Tariff-only Overall Trade Restrictiveness Index (OTRI_T), only the South Asia region had higher levels of tariff restrictiveness than MENA in 2009. The MENA region compares unfavorably with its main competitors in Europe and Central Asia, Latin America and the Caribbean, and East Asia and the Pacific—the new dynamic poles of the world economy.

Wide variations in trade restrictions exist across countries and subregions. The GCC has made tangible progress in improving backbone infrastructure and reducing trade barriers. The GCC succeeded, for example, in bringing its common external tariff down to 5 percent on most imported merchandise and to zero on essential goods. On the other hand,

North African countries continue to have prohibitive trade restrictions vis-à-vis the rest of the world. In Morocco the common weighted average import tariff in 2011 remained high at 17 percent.

Opportunities to expand trade in services vastly exceed those to expand trade in goods, and MENA countries have much to gain from services liberalization. Studies suggest that comprehensive reforms to strengthen competition and streamline regulatory frameworks would yield benefits two to three times greater than those achieved through tariff removal alone. In particular, opening up the services trade in the region would facilitate trade in parts and components and contribute to the emergence of regional production networks. At present, MENA's service exports remain dominated by tourism-related travel services of low value-added. Travel and transport together made up 78 percent of total MENA service exports in 2008. This services profile contrasts sharply with South Asia, driven by India, where information and communications technology and finance are the leading export services, making up 55 percent of service exports.

Improving Infrastructure and Cross-Border Trade Facilitation

Backbone services such as telecommunications, transport, and power are crucial to productivity and international competitiveness. Opening these sectors to competition and trade can help reduce production costs, increase FDI, promote knowledge spillovers, and expand markets, all of which enhance competitiveness. It is estimated that trade costs can constitute 20 to 40 percent of the final delivered price of MENA's nonoil exports. The cost of trade between neighbors is typically twice as high for MENA countries as in Western Europe. Maghreb countries face lower trade costs when trading with Europe than when trading among themselves. MENA's trade costs are consistently higher for agricultural products, reflecting high transportation costs (per unit value), time sensitivity for perishable products, and the impact of border controls and nontariff measures. Although some MENA countries, such as the United Arab Emirates, have excellent logistics facilities, the majority of the countries require substantial improvements in logistics and trade facilitation to bring down the high costs of trading across borders.

Backbone services also affect the region's ability to competitively export goods and services. While implementation of PAFTA has substantially reduced formal trade barriers between signatory countries, trade facilitation and transport impediments today impose greater losses in trade than formal trade tariffs and quota restrictions. Logistics and trade facilitation indicators such as the Logistics Performance Index (LPI) and Liner Shipping Connectivity Index (LSCI) show that MENA fares better in terms of connectivity than in the area of facilitation and logistics. These indicators demonstrate that the region's considerable geographical advantages are being hampered by low logistics performance and facilitation bottlenecks.

Efficient ports, maritime, and aviation services are crucial for the competitive export of goods. Most MENA countries have extensive road networks with high capacity in some areas, as well as important facilities for air and sea transport and, in several instances, a sizable rail network. Yet the quality of transport infrastructure is often deficient and unable to support growing, modern economies. Progress is being made in improving transport infrastructure. Implementation of the Mashreq Corridor Program, which aims to remove cross-border constraints, is expected to increase trade by about US$ 15 billion per year by 2020, while generating some 250,000 additional permanent jobs. Most of these jobs will be in export-oriented light manufacturing industries that typically have a higher-than-average female share of employment.

Economic integration in the power sector is at an early stage of development. Major initiatives, such as the North Africa-Middle East-Europe Mediterranean Power Pool, are taking shape, though much remains to be done to introduce competition in the power sector. Considerable progress has been made in regional integration of mobile telephony, but there are many important cross-border issues still to be tackled, particularly with regard to fixed and mobile broadband infrastructure.

Preferential Trade Agreements Have Mixed Effects

Over the past 15 years, there has been an unprecedented worldwide increase in the number, breadth, and depth of preferential trade agreements. The number of PTAs has doubled during this period, reaching 278 at the end of 2010. PTAs have been employed in all regions. Bilateral PTAs are becoming the norm, often between countries in different regions. South-South PTAs represent about two-thirds of all PTAs and North-South PTAs about one-quarter.

A large number of PTAs have been adopted in MENA over the past decade and a half, both within the region and between countries of the region, the EU, Turkey, and the United States. This proliferation of PTAs, with their varying sector and product coverage, rules of origin, and implementation requirements, constitutes a formidable implementation challenge for capacity-constrained MENA institutions. This explains, in large part, why implementation of the PTAs has been a gradual process that is still evolving.

Available evidence suggests that the implementation of PTAs has had mixed effects in MENA. The use of PTAs has contributed to a significant reduction in trade and investment barriers, provided an impetus for behind-the-border economic reforms, and helped spur rising trade (figure O.3). PTAs have also encouraged participating countries to improve their trade infrastructure, harmonize border policies and procedures, and improve their supply chains and logistics facilities. There is little evidence regarding causality between PTAs and policy reforms, however, as countries such as Egypt, Jordan, Morocco, and Tunisia have embarked on major reforms on their own. There is also no evidence that PTAs have contributed to investment flows into the region. Total FDI has risen sharply in MENA over the past decade, but the bulk of it comes from within the MENA region, essentially from the GCC. The contributions of the EU and United States have been relatively small.

The PTAs that MENA countries have signed with the EU and United States have given rise to a far more rapid expansion in imports into the region than exports out of it (figure O.3). The findings from a gravity panel model prepared for this study suggest that trade preferences granted to MENA countries by the United States, EU, and Turkey do not have an

Figure O.3   Change in PTA Volume of Trade

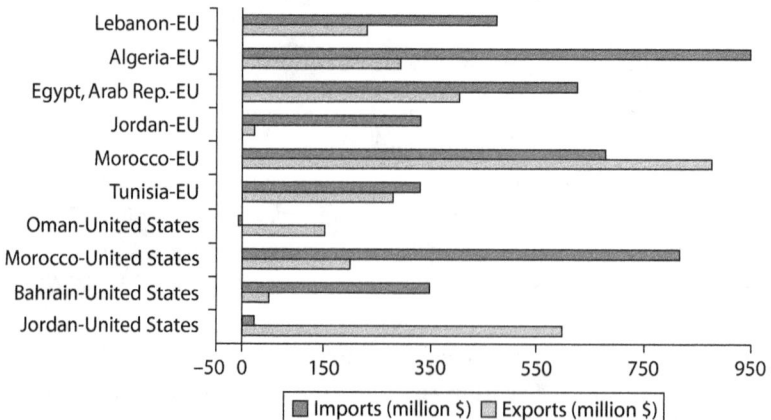

Sources: Tables C.27 and C.28.

Note: Figure represents the change from 3-year average before entry into force to 3-year average after entry into force.

additional effect on exports compared to PTAs in general (which averages about 21 percent). In fact, the additional effect is negative in the case of the EU-MENA PTA, not significant in the case of the Turkey-MENA PTA, and largely accounted for by Jordan's Qualifying Industrial Zone (QIZ) in the case of the US-MENA PTA. By contrast, PAFTA and the Agadir Agreement for the Establishment of a Free Trade Zone between Egypt, Jordan, Morocco, and Tunisia do have an additional effect in expanding the exports of their members. It should be highlighted, however, that this expansion is starting from a low intraregional trade base.

The ways in which rules of origin are calculated in different PTAs can inadvertently impede trade. Rules of origin exist in the different PTAs to preserve the value of preferences accorded to PTA members when they maintain different external tariffs. Typically, PTA members define a percentage of the value-added that must originate in another PTA member for the product to be deemed eligible for preferential tariff treatment. The rules of origin prevent products from entering the member country with lower external tariffs for transshipment to another PTA member that maintains higher tariffs against the third country's goods. As a result, the rules of origin penalize regional producers by forcing them to source from less efficient suppliers located within the region, rather than from the most competitive sources globally.

Stepping Up Policy Reforms and Political Commitment

Regional integration and global economic integration should move hand-in-hand. There are tremendous opportunities to strengthen the linkages between MENA countries and wider and deeper global markets, including through vertical integration in global production chains. Potential reforms that could deepen MENA's integration with global markets are discussed in a companion report, *From Political to Economic Awakening in the Arab World: The Path of Economic Integration, A Deauville Partnership Report on Trade and Foreign Direct Investment* (World Bank 2012).

While good progress has been made overall, with wide country variations, there remains substantial scope for further regional and global economic integration. To strengthen trade in goods, MENA countries could continue to unilaterally reduce their MFN tariffs, with an emphasis on reducing tariff peaks to the level of the most competitive regions of the world (for example, East Asia). Efforts could also be made to steadily roll back nontariff barriers to trade, which would involve reviewing existing nontariff measures, reducing their scope, and phasing out those that are not deemed essential for national security purposes.

Reforms to strengthen trade in services will be required. Such reforms would include easing entry and licensing restrictions for both domestic and foreign firms in the services sectors, promoting competition, harmonizing and strengthening regulatory practices and arrangements, and lowering restrictions on the mobility of foreign workers residing in the region. Continued public ownership in the services sectors represents a potential hurdle to increased regional cooperation, given the caution with which countries of the region have moved toward privatization. Addressing these issues would have a direct impact on employment, the overriding problem of MENA countries, as services sectors are labor-intensive and thus critical for reducing unemployment.

Within the region, continuous efforts are required to lower the costs associated with trading across borders. Reducing this burden will require measures to improve the efficiency of border-crossing points, including the harmonization of customs procedures. Logistics systems will need to be vastly improved by abolishing policies that reserve logistics activities for specific categories of domestic firms. Transport networks will need to be strengthened to improve the efficiency of ports and make better use of regional rail potential. In the power sector, institutional prerequisites for cross-border power trade need to be put in place alongside strategic investments in regional distribution and transmission networks. Opening up backbone telecommunications infrastructure to competition and encouraging inward investment in broadband services could bring information and telecommunications costs down and make Internet services more readily available.

This broad reform agenda needs to be tailored to each country's specific circumstances and stage of reform. The GCC countries have made substantial progress on reducing tariffs and nontariff measures and in improving trade logistics and infrastructure, but reforms are needed in the services area. In the Mashreq countries, which have strong links to the GCC, good infrastructure and cross-border trade facilitation should be prioritized. In the Maghreb, which has strong links to the EU, reducing tariffs and nontariff measures and cross-border trade facilitation should be high on the reform agenda.

Strong political commitment and leadership will be required if regional economic cooperation and integration are to make meaningful contributions to growth and employment in the MENA region. The political change sweeping through the Arab world provides an opportunity for the region to accelerate economic integration efforts. The Deauville initiative is timely in this regard. At its May 2011 meeting in

Deauville, France, the G8 launched a strategic partnership with countries in the MENA region undergoing political and economic change. This partnership calls on partner countries (Egypt, Jordan, Libya, Morocco, and Tunisia) to formulate homegrown economic and governance reform programs that would enhance domestic competitiveness and promote trade and FDI. In return, the Deauville partners (which include, in addition to the G8 countries, Kuwait, Qatar, Saudi Arabia, Turkey, the United Arab Emirates, and nine international and regional financial institutions) are committed to support the partner countries in achieving their goals of economic and political transformation through three strategic pillars: governance, finance, and trade and commerce.

Note

1. The LPI scores countries on six key dimensions of logistics, including the quality of trade- and transport-related infrastructure, the competence and quality of logistics services, and the efficiency of border clearance procedures. The LSCI assesses how well a country is served by container shipping services. See chapter 5 for details.

References

World Bank. 2012. *From Political to Economic Awakening in the Arab World: The Path of Economic Integration. A Deauville Partnership Report on Trade and Foreign Direct Investment.* (In two volumes). Report No. 68832-MNA. Washington, DC: World Bank.

WITS (World Integrated Trade Solution) database (2012) and World Development Indicators (2012).

CHAPTER 1

Why Economic Integration Matters: Potential Gains and Challenges

The main objective of this report is to assess the achievements in, opportunities for, and challenges of deeper regional economic cooperation and integration within the Middle East and North Africa (MENA) region and between the region and the rest of the world. Regional cooperation and global economic integration are seen in this context as two complementary processes. Stronger regional economies will have the confidence and the capacity to compete effectively on volatile and highly competitive global markets. The development of solid links between countries in a given region and larger and more affluent markets outside the region can help to raise standards and create incentives for deeper regional integration. Through this two-way feedback process between regional cooperation and economic integration, on the one hand, and global integration, on the other, each can have positive ramifications for the other.

The Arab Spring that is sweeping through the MENA region has created a sense of urgency in intensifying regional integration efforts. There are encouraging signs that new leaders are focusing on regional integration as one of several means to restoring growth, generating employment, and building more democratic and inclusive societies. For example, Tunisia recently announced its intention to reinvigorate the Arab Maghreb Union, which aims to foster cooperation among the five member countries and which had been dormant since its inception over 20 years ago. One goal of this report is to help shape the focus of the MENA region's new reform agenda.

The report is structured around four themes. First, it provides the rationale for deeper economic cooperation and integration in general, and in MENA in particular, discussing the benefits in terms of productivity gains, growth enhancement, and job creation (chapter 1). Second, it analyzes the region's performance in trading goods (chapter 2) and services (chapter 3). Third, it focuses on the importance of infrastructure (chapter 4) and behind-the-border trade facilitation (chapter 5) to regional integration. Fourth, it reviews the performance of Preferential Trade Agreements (PTAs) in MENA (chapter 6). The final chapter (chapter 7) provides a brief summary and conclusions. Two major areas left out of this study—the financial sector and education—are discussed at length in two World Bank flagship reports (Rocha, Arvai, and Farazi 2011; World Bank 2008).

The Case for Economic Integration

The MENA region's economic performance over the past three decades has been far below its potential. Despite sizable resource endowments, the region's per capita income grew by only 0.9 percent per year, on average, over the past three decades. This modest growth compares unfavorably with all other regions except Sub-Saharan Africa. While growth in per capita income picked up over the past decade to average 2.2 percent annually, and while the pace of job creation was relatively fast, unemployment has remained very high. It is estimated that the region created only 3.2 million jobs per year over the past decade—less than half the number of jobs needed. Simulation analysis suggests that average annual per capita economic growth will have to nearly double over the next decades (to about 4 percent) in order for MENA to address its employment deficit (World Bank 2011a).

The MENA region faces a number of serious economic management challenges. These include high youth unemployment, vulnerability to global commodity market shocks, water scarcity, weak governance, and inefficient public sectors. The Arab Spring has unleashed a torrent of protests across the region, giving voice to popular frustrations with exclusive, ineffective, and inefficient policy choices. The region's leaders are sensitive to the calls for reform and are accelerating measures to improve governance, stimulate job growth, make the economic growth process more inclusive, and foster popular participation in the development process (World Bank 2011b).

The political landscape in MENA is changing rapidly. Experience to date in the region suggests that like-minded political regimes tend to boost economic ties. The spread and strengthening of democratic institutions throughout the region is expected to spur broader and deeper political and economic integration among countries undergoing political reform. Blocks of countries with similar political orientations may intensify economic ties in response to growing uncertainties elsewhere. The recent move by the Gulf Cooperation Council (GCC) to expand membership to Jordan and Morocco is an example of this trend.

Meeting the MENA region's critical employment challenge will require comprehensive private sector development. The pace of job creation in the region, measured in terms of employment growth elasticity, was higher than in most other regions during the period 2004–2008. MENA's employment growth elasticity was 0.65 during this period, meaning that a 1 percent increase in gross domestic product (GDP) was associated with employment growth of 0.65 percent. Despite this growth, unemployment rates have remained high in the region, particularly for young people and women. This apparent paradox largely reflects the region's demographic realities of rapid population and labor force growth. Although a large number of new jobs are being created, formal employment is insufficient to fully absorb the large numbers of new entrants into the labor force. Consequently, many new labor force entrants are typically able to find only low-productivity and low-quality jobs in the informal sector. As indicated in a recent report (World Bank 2011c), the average MENA country produces about one-third of its GDP and employs two-thirds of its labor force informally. These are jobs without the security of tenure, benefits, or relative financial stability of formal sector jobs.

Economic integration could help policy makers address these critical development challenges. In a narrow sense, *economic integration* is understood as the elimination of tariff and nontariff barriers to the flow of goods, services, and factors of production among a group of cooperating countries. *Deeper economic integration* goes further, referring to the integration and improvement of transport and trade logistic systems, strengthening of infrastructure, harmonization of institutional arrangements and practices, and improvement in behind-the-border policies and regulations that impose a burden on business activity. The latter include economy-wide policies such as exchange rate policy, competition policy and other aspects of the overall investment climate, and sector-specific policies affecting trade in services and the efficient provision of key backbone services such as finance, transport, telecommunications, energy, and water.

Economic integration can contribute to addressing the region's development challenges by strengthening incentives and opportunities for growth, economic diversification, and employment. While it is not a panacea or a substitute for domestic reform, economic integration can help attract the investment needed to generate more and better jobs by removing barriers to trade and investment and by improving the enabling environment for both domestic and foreign investment. Global trade patterns are changing rapidly, with a growing emphasis on the geographic splintering of production chains and the rise in "trade in tasks" and vertical specialization. This has been driving trade expansion and demand for job creation in East Asia, Eastern and Central Europe, Mexico, and other parts of the world. Higher levels of intra-industry trade have generated greater and better employment for those integrated into these production chains. Despite complementarity in the output mix, nothing is preventing different countries in MENA from further integrating into these multinational value chains.

Economic integration can have positive market, efficiency, and long-term welfare effects. The extension of domestic markets provides opportunities for greater economies of scale and, through improvements in connectivity, helps strengthen access to markets. Economic integration can provide opportunities to expand economic activity through joint action to overcome policy and institutional barriers to the flow of goods, services, capital, and labor. If the reduction of interregional barriers leads partner countries to expand output and exports of internationally competitive products, the price of productive inputs or final goods in the importing country will fall and benefit consumers, input purchasers, and employees in the exporting country.

Isolation is the opposite of economic integration, and economic theory is clear on the disadvantages of small and isolated economies (Freund and Ornelas 2010; Winters 2010). Such economies have less diversified production structures and are more vulnerable to shocks than larger and more economically integrated economies. Smaller economies typically have comparatively larger public sectors because the fixed costs of government are relatively higher. Costs to private business tend to be far higher in small, isolated economies due to high trade and transport costs and limited opportunities for businesses to exploit economies of scale and scope. The source of these limited opportunities could be internal to the firms (for example, the result of small and narrow production runs) or external due to a lack of agglomeration economies. Over time, prohibitively high firm costs tend to render domestic production uncompetitive, limiting the scope for division of labor and productivity improvements (Winters 2010).

Regional and global integration are complementary processes. As mentioned above, stronger regional economies have the confidence and capacity to compete effectively on volatile and highly competitive global markets, while the development of solid links among countries in a region and between those countries and the larger and more affluent markets outside the region can help to raise standards and create incentives for deeper regional integration.

Regional integration contributes to global integration by reaping the benefits of geographical proximity, promoting learning by doing, and fostering competitiveness. As regional integration proceeds, the need for better domestic infrastructure and cross-border trading arrangements will become more apparent. Investment in cross-border infrastructure and trade facilitation services will, in turn, boost competitiveness, preparing the countries of the region to compete in global markets. To ensure that regional integration is indeed complementary to globalization, many MENA countries have encouraged "open regionalism," which implies negotiating reciprocal preferences with regional partners while simultaneously opening up to international markets.

Conversely, global integration can provide added pressure on countries to improve integration within their region. Positive neighborhood effects occur when countries in a region are integrated into global trade and investment flows. Not only will global economic integration bolster competitiveness and lower costs, but also it will induce countries to adopt policies and institutional arrangements that are necessary for doing business in competitive global markets.

Within a given region, economic integration can lead to efficiency gains and boost productivity. This is the result of reducing time and operating costs (through lower physical barriers to trade), reducing nonphysical barriers to trade (for example, by lowering transaction costs due to harmonized customs, trade facilitation, and border formalities), and reducing the cost of and improving access to new knowledge and to production factors (such as power supply, capital, and skilled labor). Opening up domestic markets through regional economic integration can increase competition in sectors with highly concentrated industrial structures.

The procompetitive effects of cross-border economic integration are particularly important in countries with concentrated industrial sectors and limited domestic competition policies.

Regional economic integration can also have important learning effects. Opening up markets on a preferential basis can help export-oriented firms learn how to enter foreign markets and find overseas customers and suppliers. Exposing import-competing firms to foreign competition can force them to boost their competitiveness, which may in turn prepare them to compete in global markets. Regional economic integration efforts can also serve as a training ground for policy makers in negotiating highly technical aspects of trade and investment agreements.

By setting standards for good institutional practice, regional integration can contribute to good governance and accelerate institutional transformation. Adopting common customs procedures, domestic investment rules and regulations, and product quality standards can boost foreign domestic investment inflows and enhance the credibility of domestic investment regimes. Regional integration efforts can also help to reinforce positive policy reform efforts by anchoring reforms within a multiparty agreement, thus making it more difficult for domestic lobby groups to reverse policy reforms as a means to preserve or enhance their economic rents.

The process of regional economic integration poses both political challenges and opportunities. If successful, integration is likely to spur the movement of people, capital, and enterprises, which may be of concern to national policy makers. Regional economic integration implies forgoing some of the member countries' rights to set their own standards and policies, which may be difficult for national political leaders to accept. Yet, at the same time, regional economic integration can help lock in desirable reforms and keep special interest groups from lobbying policy makers to act unilaterally. By linking the fortunes of economies in a geographic region through trade, investment, and factor flows, regional economic integration can be seen as an investment in soft security, multiplying the number of stakeholders who have a vested interest in resolving conflicts amicably.

International experience suggests that progress in economic integration is linked directly to achieving "early wins," building widespread awareness of the potential benefits of economic integration, and maintaining strong political support for economic integration (De Melo 2008; Hill and Menon 2010; Olarreaga 2008). Successful efforts to integrate economies have often followed the development of cross-country supplier networks. For example, in Eastern Europe's automobile industry, and in East Asia's electronics, natural resources, and petrochemical sectors, these networks have contributed significantly to economic success in these regions. Such cross-border production networks are able to take advantage of inter-country wage and natural resource endowment differentials, short trans-port distances, and economies of scale arising from specialization. These production chains are evolving, with different countries coming to play different roles in the value chains as national competencies and capacities change. In Asia, for example, as economies have become integrated through trade, financial flows, and direct investment, intraregional trade has grown to the point where Asia trades about as much with itself as Europe and North America do with themselves (box 1.1) (Asian Development Bank 2008, 2010; Barro and Lee 2011; International Customs Union 2009). There are signs that MENA nations are starting to integrate into global production chains. Morocco, for example, has devel-oped assembly operations and processing plants as part of the global automotive industry. There remains considerable scope in MENA for integrating into global production chains for industrial products, particularly in labor-abundant countries.

If not managed appropriately, economic integration efforts could foster inefficiency. This outcome could arise from diverting trade, bolstering protectionism, enabling special interest groups to lobby governments to form distortionary agreements, and discouraging integration with global economies. Ultimately, badly designed integration efforts could boost costs, reduce competitiveness, and hamper growth.

The costs and benefits of economic integration are not the same for all MENA countries, which explains why integration priorities tend to vary within the region. For some MENA countries, the greatest potential ben-efits come from integrating more closely with a small number of neigh-boring economies. For others, the most significant potential benefits emanate from integrating national economies with others at a subregional or regional level. In addition, considerable efforts have been made in recent years to foster economic integration between MENA countries and the EU and the United States, both major trade and investment partners.

The potential costs and benefits of regional integration are an empirical matter: Economic theory, as discussed above, suggests that there can be considerable benefits, although they might be costly to achieve. The following chapters examine various aspects of economic

Box 1.1

ASEAN–A Model of Open Regionalism

The 10-member Association of Southeast Asian Nations (ASEAN) was established in August 1967. Beginning in 1976, with its five original members, ASEAN began to move toward economic cooperation and integration, initially with a focus on merchandise trade. In the 1990s, it expanded its focus to include services, investment, and labor. And in the past decade—now including all of Southeast Asia—ASEAN broadened cooperation on macroeconomic and financial issues, many of these together with its Northeast Asian neighbors—the "Plus 3," including China, Japan, and the Republic of Korea. Members adopted what may appear to be formal PTAs, but in practice these were usually multilateralized, as ASEAN informally embraces what is sometimes termed "open regionalism."

The payoffs from ASEAN integration have been substantial. The total trade-to-GDP ratio of ASEAN nations has increased from 20 percent in the 1960s to an average of 140 percent in the first decade of the 2000s, far surpassing the European Union (EU) as the world's most trade-oriented region. Trade within ASEAN has increased from 4 percent of GDP in the mid-1960s to an average of 35 percent of GDP 40 years later.

Over time, a unique nexus of trade and investment flows developed in the ASEAN region, connecting the region's wealthier and poorer countries and creating strong regional production networks and a vibrant regional economy. This cross-border collaboration involves shipments of raw materials as well as manufacturing parts and components that crisscross the region, along with foreign investment and skilled labor. In 2005–06, for example, parts and components accounted for 44 percent of ASEAN-manufactured exports, up from 29 percent in 1992–93. The shares are higher still for some countries: 64 percent for the Philippines in 2005–06 (up from 24 percent in 1992–93), 53 percent in Singapore (up from 32 percent), and 51 percent in Malaysia (up from 37 percent). Protectionism has been slashed. As of 2009, zero tariffs applied to 64 percent of products in the Inclusion List of ASEAN+6 (ASEAN+3 plus Australia, India, and New Zealand). The average tariff is down to 1.5 percent, from 12.8 percent when tariff cutting began in 1993.

Sources: Capannelli, Lee, and Petri 2009; Hill and Menon 2010.

integration in MENA, with an emphasis on assessing what has been accomplished to date, examining the impediments to advancing economic integration, and identifying the benefits that deeper economic integration could bring.

References

Asian Development Bank. 2008. *Emerging Asian Regionalism: A Partnership for Shared Prosperity*. Manila: Asian Development Bank.

———. 2010. *Institutions for Regional Integration: Toward an Asian Economic Community*. Manila: Asian Development Bank.

Barro, Robert J., and Jong-Wha Lee. 2011. *Costs and Benefits of Economic Integration in Asia*. New York: Oxford University Press.

Capannelli, Giovanni, Jong-Wha Lee, and Peter Petri. 2009. *Developing Indicators for Regional Economic Integration and Cooperation*. Manila: Asian Development Bank.

De Melo, Jaime. 2008. "Lessons from COMESA Integration for PAFTA." Paper prepared for the Seminar on Strengthening the Pan Arab Free Trade Area, Oman, May 2008.

Freund, Caroline, and Emanuel Ornelas. 2010. "Regional Trade Agreements." *Annual Review of Economics* 2 (1): 139.

Hill, Hal, and Jayant Menon. 2010. "ASEAN Economic Integration: Features, Fulfillments, Failures and the Future." ADB Working Paper Series on Regional Economic Integration, Asian Development Bank, Manila.

International Customs Union. 2009. "Regional Cooperation and Economic Integration: Challenges and Opportunities." Proceedings of the Third International Conference, Skopje, Republic of Macedonia, October 15–17.

Olarreaga, Marcelo. 2008. "Regionalism: A View from Mercosur." Paper prepared for the Seminar on Strengthening the Pan Arab Free Trade Area. Oman.

Rocha, Roberto R., Zsofia Arvai, and Subika Farazi. 2011. *Financial Access and Stability: A Road Map for the Middle East and North Africa*. MENA Financial Sector Flagship. Washington, DC: World Bank.

Winters, L. Alan. 2010. "Regional Integration and Small Countries in South Asia." In *Accelerating Growth and Job Creation in South Asia*, ed. Ejaz Ghani and Sadiq Ahmed, 291–342. New Delhi: Oxford University Press.

World Bank. 2008. *The Road Not Traveled: Education Reform in the Middle East and North Africa*. MENA Development Report. Washington, DC: World Bank.

———. 2011a. *Investing for Growth and Jobs: World Bank Middle East and North Africa Region Economic Developments and Prospects*. Washington, DC: World Bank.

————. 2011b. "Towards a New Partnership for Inclusive Growth in the Middle East and North Africa." Arab World Brief No. 5 (May). Washington, DC: World Bank.

————. 2011c. "Striving for Better Jobs: The Challenge of Informality in the Middle East and North Africa." MENA Knowledge and Learning Quick Notes No. 49. Washington, DC: World Bank.

CHAPTER 2

Regional Integration through Trade in Goods

This chapter discusses the Middle East and North Africa (MENA) region's achievements in and constraints to regional trade integration in goods. It proposes some actions that can be taken to further trade within and outside the region. The chapter draws on and updates existing work carried out by the World Bank, namely, Chauffour (2011), Rouis (2010), Rouis and Al-Abdulrazzaq (2010), and Rouis and Kounetsron (2010). In particular, this report complements the findings of the Deauville Partnership Report on Trade and Foreign Direct Investment, which was requested by the G8 (Deauville Request) through the Marseille Center for Mediterranean Integration (World Bank 2012). The Deauville report focuses on boosting Arab integration in the global economy by adopting policies that foster improved market access and regulations; competitiveness, diversification, and employment; trade facilitation, trade finance, and remittances; and inclusiveness, equity, and sustainability.

Trade Performance

Trade volumes in MENA have increased sharply as competitiveness has improved and demand for the region's main exports has increased. From the late 1990s to the late 2000s, total MENA exports have more than quadrupled, rising from US$ 194 billion per year to US$ 825 billion per year. Total imports have increased from US$ 165 billion per year to US$ 607 billion per year (table C.3). Some 80 percent of the growth in exports is accounted for by petroleum, and the region's petroleum-exporting countries accounted for two-thirds of the growth in import demand. These figures underscore the important role played by petroleum, the region's most competitive product, in external trade.

Trade integration with the global economy has been relatively slow in the MENA region. Though home to 5.5 percent of the world's population (on average for 2008–10) and 3.9 percent of the world's gross domestic product (GDP), the region's share of nonoil world trade is only 1.8 percent. The region's share had remained below 1 percent for a long time and started to increase gradually only during the past decade. There are slight variations among subregions, and there are wide intercountry variations, with Tunisia and Morocco exhibiting higher trade volumes and export diversification. Most of the countries have a narrow trade base, however, and—outside of petroleum—very low (2–3 percent of total trade) merchandise trade within the region (Hoekman and Zarrouk 2009).

The Gulf Cooperation Council (GCC) nations have taken the lead in global economic integration in the past decade, rapidly expanding trade and investment links with China and India on the basis of strong complementarity with these countries (Habibi 2011). China and India are the fastest-growing oil consumers in the world, and the GCC countries have the largest deposits of oil and gas. The sharp increase in bilateral trade has been dominated by Saudi Arabia and the United Arab Emirates. Exports from the GCC to India and China are dominated by fossil fuels. Imports into the GCC from India are dominated by food and refined products, and those from China by manufactured consumer goods and capital goods. Rapid growth in merchandise trade has also triggered growth in bilateral investments, notably in the energy, real estate, and finance sectors.

Though on a rising trend, integration within the MENA region remains low, particularly compared with other middle- and high-income regions of the world. Intraregional exports have averaged less than 8 percent of total exports in the MENA region over the period 2008–10, as compared to 25 percent in ASEAN and 66 percent in the European Union (EU) (table C.13). There is wide country variation within the MENA region, with the Maghreb countries accounting for the lowest share of total exports and the Mashreq countries for the highest share—more than three times that of the Maghreb (table C.5).

The picture is largely similar for nonoil merchandise exports. At less than 5 percent, the Maghreb countries represent the lowest share of intraregional nonoil merchandise trade (figure 2.1). This share has increased only marginally since 2000. Intraregional trade in the Mashreq and GCC represents a somewhat larger share of trade. In the Syrian Arab Republic and the Republic of Yemen, regional markets account for more than half of all nonoil exports. In Bahrain, Lebanon, Oman, and the United Arab Emirates, they account for 35–40 percent and comprise more than 25 percent of nonoil exports in the Arab Republic of Egypt, Jordan, Kuwait, and Saudi Arabia. The ratio of intraregional trade to GDP exceeds 15 percent in Jordan and Syria, but remains in the low single digits in the other MENA countries. It remains particularly low in resource-rich, labor-importing countries, where the ratio of total exports to GDP is high (Hoekman and Zarrouk 2009).

The level of MENA countries' participation in vibrant global production networks could be described as negligible. Intra-industry trade is low, reaching just 20 percent of manufacturing in countries such as Egypt—far below the 70 percent share found in China and other East Asian countries. Component trade is minimal, reflecting the low technology content of the region's imports and exports. As a result, the MENA region has been unable to benefit from the knowledge spillovers that tend to occur in global production networks.

Figure 2.1   Export Share by Destination (Excluding Oil)

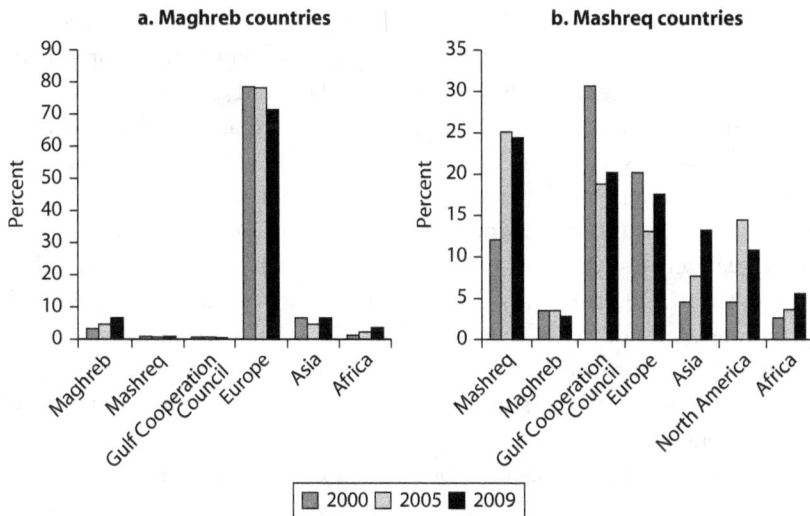

Source: UN Comtrade Statistics 2012.

MENA countries face stiff competition from the rise of China and India in global trade. While demand from these countries is rising, competition for traditional nonoil export markets is increasing steadily, making it more difficult for MENA countries to retain market share. For example, China's share of the EU market has risen dramatically over the past decade, particularly in the markets for textiles, apparel, and electronics. In 1995 the EU was the dominant market for Maghreb countries' exports, accounting for at least three-quarters of exports. The EU market accounted for about half of exports from Egypt, Islamic Republic of Iran, and Syria. By 2006, however, the EU's share had fallen in every Maghreb country except the Republic of Yemen. On the home front, rapidly growing imports from China and India have lowered consumer prices in the MENA region, increasing the competition faced by domestic producers, particularly in the electronics, textiles, leather, and furniture industries (Pigato 2009).

Various factors contribute to low levels of trade integration. A number of MENA countries have similar resource endowments, production capabilities, and export structures. They may find it difficult to use regional integration as a means to establish patterns of specialization and diversification. The lack of intraregional trade is also, to some extent, driven by policy. As analyzed in a recent World Bank publication, public sector governance and participation, accountability and transparency, and rents and privileges remain key impediments to private sector development in the region (World Bank 2009).

A narrow export base is both a cause and a consequence of low integration in regional and global commodity markets. The MENA region as a whole is characterized by exports of primary commodities, largely oil and gas (76 percent in 2008–10). Manufactured goods account for 11.4 percent, and other sectors account for the remaining 13 percent.

While MENA countries' exports are highly concentrated and less diversified overall, they have seen some improvement in the last 15 years. In 2010, five countries (Egypt, Jordan, Lebanon, Morocco, and Tunisia) were relatively less concentrated than the rest, with a concentration index of less than 0.2 (figure 2.2). Three other countries (Bahrain, Syria, and the United Arab Emirates) had an index below 0.4. While most countries made some improvements in export diversification during this time period, the level of diversification remains quite low compared to the world average.

MENA countries have underperformed other countries with similar income levels in developing new exports. Exports are generally produced

Figure 2.2   Concentration and Diversification Indices of Export Products in MENA

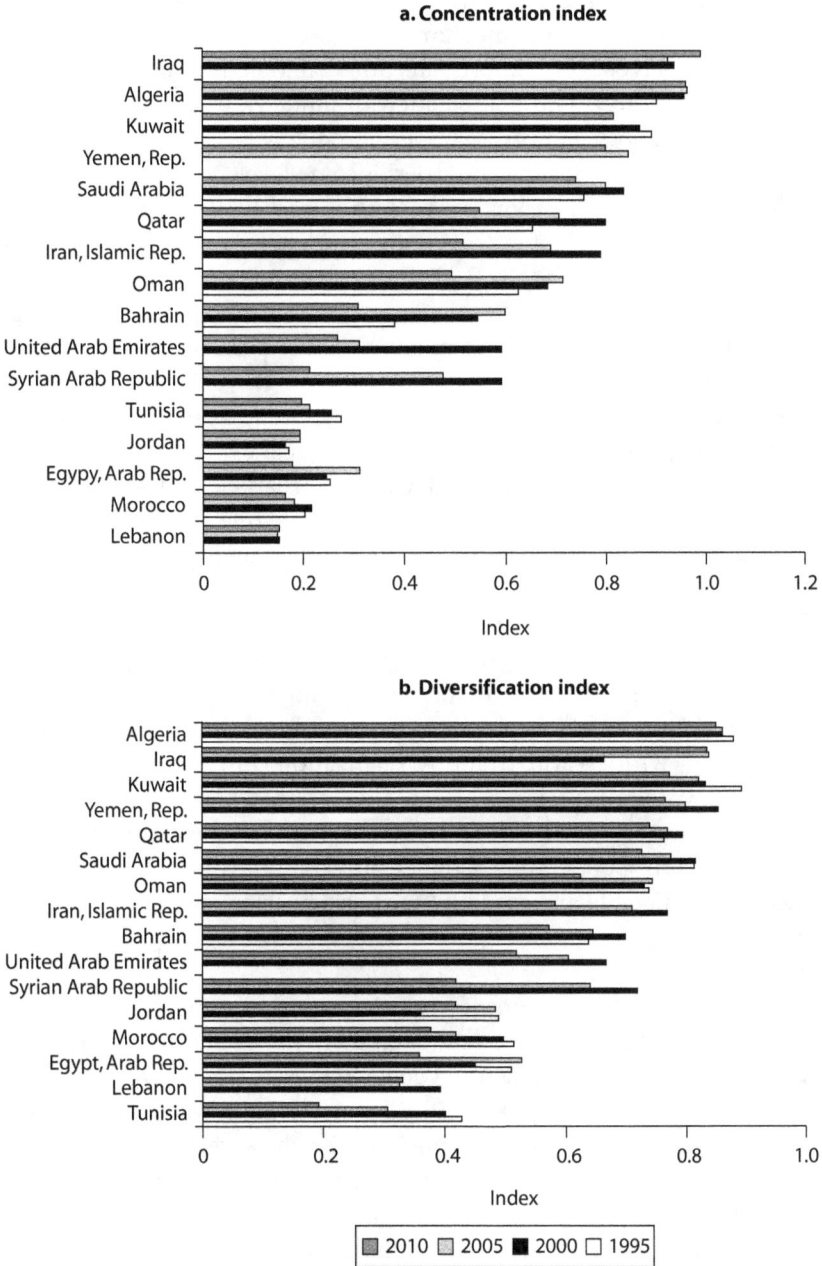

a. Concentration index

b. Diversification index

■ 2010 ▨ 2005 ■ 2000 ☐ 1995

Source: UN Comtrade Statistics 2011.

with low levels of skill and are unsophisticated. For example, only 21 percent of total exports from Egypt, Jordan, Lebanon, Morocco, and Tunisia are classified as medium- or high-technology, compared with almost 37 percent of exports in other middle-income economies (World Bank 2009). This combination of limited export diversification and low-technology industry hampers productivity growth in MENA, which is already low for the countries' income levels.

In addition to high export concentration and limited diversification, the technology content of exports is low. Evidence shows that the nature of exports affects growth (box 2.1). There are encouraging signs in at least two countries, Jordan and Tunisia, where high-tech exports are gaining momentum, though evolving from a low base and, in the case of Jordan, a narrow base.

Industrial policies have contributed to the MENA region's progress in improving the sophistication of technological exports, as illustrated by Jordan's pharmaceutical industry and Tunisia's electronics industry. Well-crafted industrial policies have played a role, as illustrated by Tunisia's decision in the 1990s to abandon the manufacturing of cars and focus instead on manufacturing components in partnership with European automakers. Both countries established an "enclave" where transparent "rules of the game" were credibly enforced—specifically, Tunisia's offshore regime and Jordan's Qualifying Industrial Zone. In addition, Jordan's free trade agreement with the United States and compliance with World Trade Organization Intellectual Property Rights provisions gave investors confidence that high-tech processes would be protected. These observations point to the importance of economic Gulf Cooperation Council integration as a force for introducing a predictable and credible trade and business environment, and the role it plays in upgrading the quality of exports (Diop and Ghali, Forthcoming).

Exports from GCC countries remain highly concentrated in a few commodities, largely oil and gas, though there has been some diversification in recent years. Manufactured goods represent a much higher share in Bahrain (19 percent in 2008–10). Manufacturing exports play a more important role in the Mashreq countries, with the exception of Iraq, and account for 73 percent of exports in Jordan, 60 percent in Lebanon, and 39 percent in Syria (appendix C, table C.17).

Within the Maghreb subregion, some countries have a narrow range of exports while others export a wider variety of product lines. Algeria and Libya export almost nothing but fuels, whereas Tunisia and

Box 2.1

Moving Up the Technological Ladder in Exports—The Cases of Jordan and Tunisia

Exports from MENA countries tend to be narrowly based and characterized by low technological sophistication. The low-tech nature of MENA exports is problematic in a number of respects. First, there is evidence that what countries export matters for growth. Hausmann, Hwang, and Rodrik (2007) show that the extent to which a country's export basket overlaps with the goods exported by richer countries is a significant predictor of the country's growth rate. In earlier papers, Fagerberg (1988) and Dalum, Laursen, and Verspagen (1999) stress that exporting products with higher income elasticity—typically the case of technology-intensive products—provides better growth prospects. In the same vein, Lall (2000) argues that low-technology products tend to grow the slowest and technology-intensive products the fastest. Finally, to the extent that technology-intensive sectors are more productive, moving resources into these sectors enhances productivity and competitiveness. A rise in productivity is particularly important for the competitiveness of countries with a large middle class and rising wages.

Jordan and Tunisia are among the few MENA countries that have managed to boost the technological content of their merchandise exports. High-tech exports in Jordan, which now account for 10.3 percent of total exports, are driven almost exclusively (98.6 percent) by pharmaceutical products. Jordan's pharmaceutical sector offers significant value-added for the economy, with strong links to local input markets (such as packaging, material capsules, technology, and research) and an ability to add real or perceived value to the products through branding. High-quality products are exported to more than 60 markets worldwide, which attests to their competitiveness, particularly with regard to generic drugs.

Tunisia moved up the technological ladder slowly but steadily from a low base. The shares of high- and medium-tech exports have increased as a percentage of total exports (reaching 6.5 and 41.2 percent, respectively, in 2009), while exports of low-tech products have declined significantly (to 38.3 percent). Unlike Jordan, Tunisia has a broad high-tech export base (including electrical wiring systems, electrical motors and generators, wheels and rubber tires, plastic auto components, and mechanical auto parts), with electrical wiring systems by far the most dynamic subsector. Tunisia is now among Europe's top ten suppliers in that subsector.

Source: Diop and Ghali, forthcoming.

Morocco export a large share of manufactured goods (74 and 63 percent, respectively), including chemicals, machinery, and equipment parts in 2008–10.[1]

Barriers to Trade in Goods Have Been Reduced to Some Extent

Significant progress has been made in reducing barriers to trade in goods within the MENA region and, to some extent, between the region and the rest of the world. Over the last decade, preferential liberalization under the Pan Arab Free Trade Area (PAFTA) and other PTAs has been complemented by reductions in most favored nation (MFN) tariffs. As a result, the average uniform tariff equivalent of all tariffs (*ad valorem* and specific) for the region fell from 14.7 percent in 2002 to 6.7 percent in 2007, and by another 0.8 percentage points during 2008–09, despite the global economic crisis. In fact, MENA was the region where tariffs decreased the most during the financial crisis, especially on manufacturing goods (Chauffour and Maur 2010). Egypt, for example, reduced its weighted average tariff from 19.3 percent in 2005 to 6.3 percent in 2008. The GCC succeeded in bringing its common external tariff down to 5 percent on most imported merchandise and to 0 percent on essential goods (comprising some 400 items). In Morocco, however, the common weighted average import tariff remained high in 2011 at 17 percent.

Notwithstanding progress made in the last decade, the level of tariff protection in the MENA region vis-à-vis the rest of the world remains high by international standards. According to the Tariff-only Overall Trade Restrictiveness Index (OTRI_T),[2] only the South Asia region had higher levels of tariff restrictiveness than MENA in 2009 (figure 2.3). The MENA region compares unfavorably with its main competitors in Europe and Central Asia, Latin America and the Caribbean, and East Asia and the Pacific—the new dynamic poles of the world economy. In particular, agriculture in the MENA region is still relatively heavily protected by high tariffs. With comparatively small domestic markets, trade and investment liberalization is crucial for integrating the region into production-sharing or processing types of trade, through which each country specializes in areas of comparative advantage and factor endowment to serve bigger markets. This situation will materialize only if there is a substantial increase in the efficiency of logistics and other trade services.

Figure 2.3   Tariff-only Overall Trade Restrictiveness Index (OTRI_T) by Region, 2009

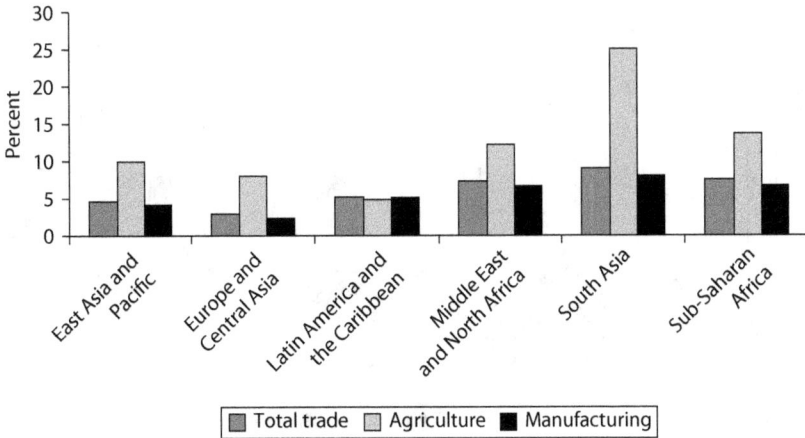

Source: Kee, Neagu, and Nicita, forthcoming.

Nontariff measures (NTMs) have become the most important barriers to trade in the MENA region. Despite tariff liberalization under PAFTA, NTMs continue to impede regional integration. In addition to border closures, these NTMs include excessive delays resulting from lengthy clearance and inspection processes, the number of documents and signatures needed to process a trade transaction, and the frequency of problems with customs and other government authorities. When NTMs are included in the calculation of the OTRI,[3] the MENA region comes across as the most restrictive region in the world, driven by high NTMs on agriculture goods (figure 2.4). The only exception is South Asia for agriculture.

The pervasiveness of NTMs is compounded by relatively poor regional trade logistics performance. Data on the performance of logistics services and on the internal costs associated with shipping goods from the factory gate to the port, and from ports to retail outlets, suggest that traders confront significant hurdles in the region, with only the United Arab Emirates being among the world's better performers. The *Doing Business* "cost of trading" data indicate that the costs associated with completing the procedures to export or import a 20-foot container (including document and administrative fees for customs clearance and technical control, terminal handling charges, and inland transport) remain high in MENA (table 2.1).[4] Only Qatar, Saudi Arabia, and the United Arab Emirates were among the top 40 logistics performers in 2012. The Logistics

Figure 2.4   Overall Trade Restrictiveness Index (OTRI) by Region, 2009

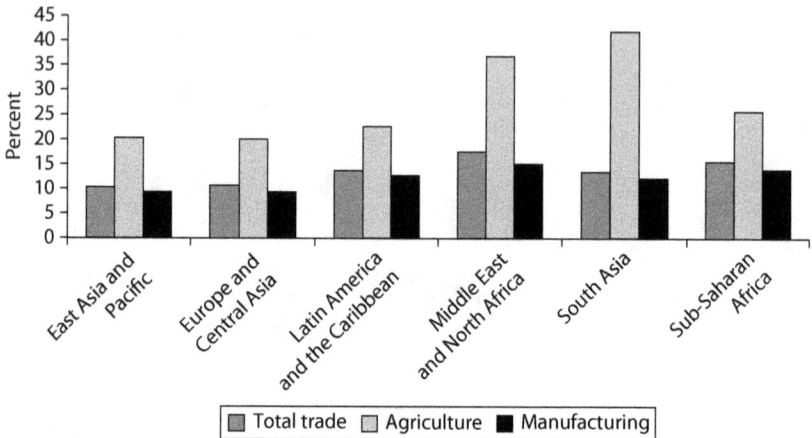

Source: Kee, Neagu, and Nicita, forthcoming.

Table 2.1   Trading across MENA Borders

Country	Rank	Country	Rank	Country	Rank
GCC	48	Resource-rich	125	Resource-poor	53
Bahrain	49	Algeria	127	Djibouti	37
Kuwait	112	Egypt, Arab Rep.	64	Jordan	58
Oman	47	Iran, Islamic Rep.	138	Lebanon	93
Qatar	57	Iraq	180	Morocco	43
Saudi Arabia	18	Syrian Arab Republic	122	Tunisia	32
United Arab Emirates	5	Yemen, Rep.	118		

Source: International Finance Corporation 2011.

Performance Index (LPI) reveals a great deal of variation and significant performance bottlenecks within many MENA countries (figure 2.5).[5] Performance in the predominantly high-income Gulf states is noticeably stronger. The standout performer is the United Arab Emirates, which ranks 17th in the world on the 2012 LPI with a score comparable to that of Australia and Switzerland.

Policy Recommendations

Despite the gains made thus far, there *continue* to be significant opportunities to reform trade regimes in MENA so as to foster closer economic integration. In the years to come, MENA countries could continue to

Figure 2.5   LPI Scores in MENA versus Other Regions

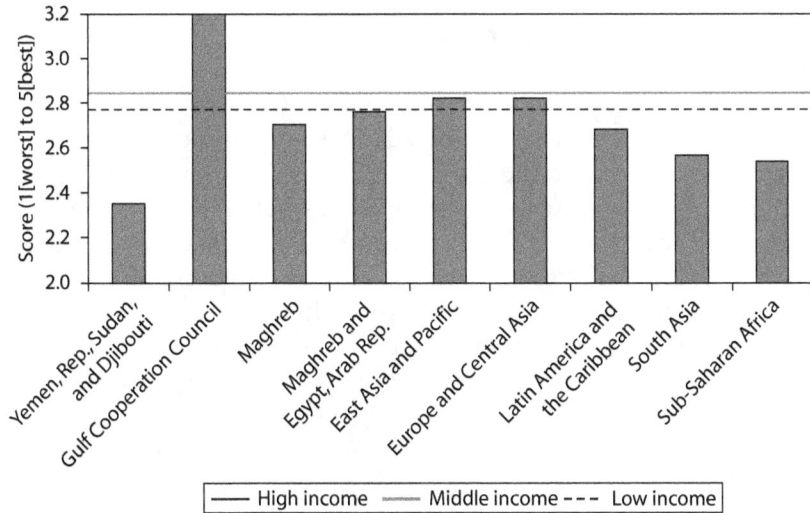

Source: Logistics Performance Index 2012.

unilaterally reduce their MFN tariffs, especially tariff peaks, to the level of the most competitive regions of the world (for example, East Asia). Unilateral liberalization has proven to be a successful strategy in a number of emerging trading partners that are now sustainable growth poles. Efforts could also be made to reduce all nontariff barriers to trade in the region. This would involve reviewing existing NTMs, streamlining them on the basis of lessons learned from other countries around the world, and establishing regulatory impact assessments to improve the process through which new NTMs are created.

There is also a need to strengthen mechanisms for tracking and enforcing commitments to liberalize trade within the region. In Arab countries, a stronger mandate could be given to a dedicated and independent PAFTA Secretariat endowed with skilled staff, as in the case of the Common Market for Eastern and Southern Africa (COMESA) Secretariat. This entity would be entrusted to monitor the implementation of PAFTA members' liberalization commitments, including the dismantlement of NTMs and the liberalization of services. The secretariat could play an instrumental role in devising a service negotiation strategy that is comprehensive for the regional bloc yet customized to each of the PAFTA members' needs and goals. Regular monitoring of implementation commitments would be important to allow policy makers to assess the effects of the agreement. Adopting simple rules of origin should be considered to encourage countries in the region to trade with each other, and to source imports from the most competitive supply points.

To realize the goals of establishing an Arab Customs Union by 2015 and an Arab Common Market by 2020, efforts will need to be made to strengthen the rules and discipline applicable to PAFTA and other regional institutions. Achieving these goals would involve strengthening or agreeing on a new set of basic principles for the governance of PAFTA, including the prohibition of NTMs, unless they fulfill criteria such as nondiscrimination and necessity, effective national treatment provisions in the services trade, and an effective framework to guarantee the free movement of labor within the region. This would also involve creating a permanent and independent dispute settlement mechanism to oversee enforcement, including measures to ensure compliance.

Notes

1. Achy (2006) shows the pattern of exports for 2004. Algeria and Libya's fuel exports account for 96 and 95 percent of total exports, respectively. Mauritania is dependent on the export of minerals and metals (40 percent). Morocco and Tunisia are slightly more diversified, but with high concentration in the export of manufactured products (67 and 78 percent, respectively).

2. The OTRI_T is calculated as a weighted sum of *ad valorem* tariffs and the *ad valorem* equivalent of specific duties, where the weights are import volumes and import demand elasticities. See Kee, Neagu, and Nicita (Forthcoming) for details.

3. The OTRI adds NTMs to the OTRI_T to calculate an OTRI. See Kee, Neagu, and Nicita (forthcoming) for details.

4. The cost measure does not include tariffs or trade taxes. Only official costs are recorded. Inland transport costs are based on distance to the shipping port. The methodology, surveys, and data are available at http://www.doingbusiness.org.

5. The LPI is based on a worldwide survey of operators on the ground (global freight forwarders and express carriers), providing feedback on the logistics "friendliness" of the countries in which they operate and those with which they trade. The methodology, surveys, and data are available at http://www.worldbank.org/lpi.

References

Achy, Lahcen. 2006. *Assessing Regional Integration Potential in North Africa in trade in North Africa*. United Nations Economic Commission for Africa Report, ECA Office for North Africa, Rabat.

Chauffour, Jean-Pierre. 2011. "Trade Integration as a Way Forward for the Arab World: A Regional Agenda." World Bank Policy Research Working Paper No. 5581, World Bank, Washington, DC.

Chauffour, Jean-Pierre, and Jean-Christopher Maur. 2010. "Beyond Market Access: The New Normal of Preferential Trade Agreements." Policy Research Working Paper No. 5454, World Bank, Washington, DC.

Dalum, B., K. Laursen, and B. Verspagen. 1999. "Does Specialization Matter for Growth?" *Industrial and Corporate Change* 8: 267–88.

Diop, Ndiamé, and Sofiane Ghali. Forthcoming. "Globalization and the Dynamic Evolution of the Quality of Exports: Are Jordan and Tunisia Moving Up the Technological Ladder?"

Fagerberg, Jan Ernst. 1988. "International Competitiveness." *Economic Journal* 98 (June): 355–74.

Habibi, Nader. 2011. "Growth in Economic Relations of China and India with the GCC Countries." *Asian-Pacific Economic Literature* 25 (2): 52–67.

Hausmann, Ricardo, Jason Hwang, and Dani Rodrik. 2007. "What You Export Matters." *Journal of Economic Growth* 12 (1): 1–25.

Hoekman, Bernard, and Jemal Zarrouk. 2009. "Changes in Cross-Border Trade Costs in Pan Arab Free Trade Area." Policy Research Working Paper No. 5031, World Bank, Washington, DC.

International Finance Corporation. 2011. *Doing Business 2011*. Washington, DC: World Bank.

Kee, Hiau Looi, Cristina Neagu, and Alessandro Nicita. Forthcoming. "Is Protectionism on the Rise? Assessing National Trade Policies during the Crisis of 2008." *Review of Economics and Statistics*.

Lall, Sanjaya. 2000. "The Technological Structure and Performance of Developing Country Manufactured Exports, 1985–98." *Oxford Development Studies* 28 (3): 337–69.

Logistics Performance Index. 2012. World Bank, Washington, DC. http://go.worldbank.org/7TEVSUEARO.

Pigato, Miria. 2009. *Strengthening China's and India's Trade and Investment Ties to the Middle East and North Africa*. Orientations in Development Series. Washington, DC: World Bank.

Rouis, Mustapha. 2010. *Economic Integration in the Mashreq*. Middle East and North Africa Region. Washington, DC: World Bank.

Rouis, Mustapha, and Ali Al-Abdulrazzaq. 2010. *Economic Integration in the GCC.* Middle East and North Africa Region. Washington DC: The World Bank.

Rouis, Mustapha, and Komlan Kounetsron. 2010. *Economic Integration in the Maghreb.* Middle East and North Africa Region. Washington, DC: World Bank.

UN Comtrade Statistics. 2012.

World Bank. 2009. *From Privilege to Competition: Unlocking Private-Led Growth.* MENA Development Report. Washington, DC: World Bank.

———. 2012. *From Political to Economic Awakening in the Arab World: The Path of Economic Integration. A Deauville Partnership Report on Trade and Foreign Direct Investment.* (In two volumes). Report No. 68832-MNA. Washington, DC: World Bank.

CHAPTER 3

Regional Integration through Trade in Services

The services sector in Middle East and North Africa (MENA) represents an average of 46 percent of gross domestic product (GDP), with wide variations across countries. Though it has increased over time, this share remains low by international comparison (see figure 3.3, page 32) and smaller than would be predicted by the region's income levels. There is tremendous scope for expanding services trade, but success in this area will require deep beyond-the-border reforms that make it possible for companies to operate seamlessly across national boundaries. Services trade typically involves skilled individuals establishing operations in new markets. For this to occur, the regulatory framework must be conducive to cross-border flows of capital, technology, and skilled labor. This chapter discusses the role of trade in services, impediments to services trade, progress made in opening up the region to services trade, and the role of regional trade agreements in boosting trade in services.

In spite of its comparatively small size, the services sector has been a key source of growth and wealth creation in MENA. The average annual growth of services value-added stood at 5.2 percent during the period 2000–10, as compared to 4.5 percent for overall economic growth. The positive relationship between the growth of real per-capita GDP and the growth of services value-added in MENA countries (figure 3.1) implies

Figure 3.1   Services Value-Added Growth Is Positively Correlated with Per-Capita GDP Growth in MENA

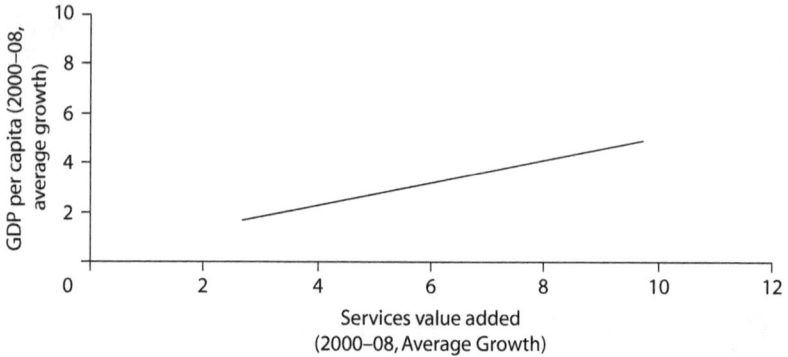

Source: World Development Indicators 2012.

that MENA countries with high growth in services tend to have higher national incomes or, conversely, that countries with high overall economic growth also have high service-sector growth.

The dynamism of the services sectors in MENA countries pales in comparison to countries in East Asia, South Asia, and, to a lesser degree, Europe and Central Asia. The services sectors in these regions grew, on average, by 9.5, 8.3, and 5.4 percent, respectively, during the period 2000–10. Despite doubling its services exports, MENA's share in total global services trade has stagnated at around 2 to 3 percent during the past decade.

Services Trade Performance

Along with Latin America and Sub-Saharan Africa, MENA is a relatively minor player in the global trade of information and communications technology, finance, and other business services. The services trade in MENA grew by 12.4 percent annually during 2000–08, compared to 23 percent in South Asia, 16 percent in East Asia, and 14 percent in Europe and Central Asia. MENA's share in the global services trade stagnated at around 2.8 percent between 2000 and 2008 (Borchert, Demartino, and Mattoo 2010).

The region's lack of dynamism in services exports reflects its low value-added orientation. Exports of services remain dominated by tourism-related travel services. In 2008 this category accounted for 53 percent of total services exports. Travel and transport together made up 78 percent

Figure 3.2   Export Composition

a. MENA, 2008	b. South Asia, 2008

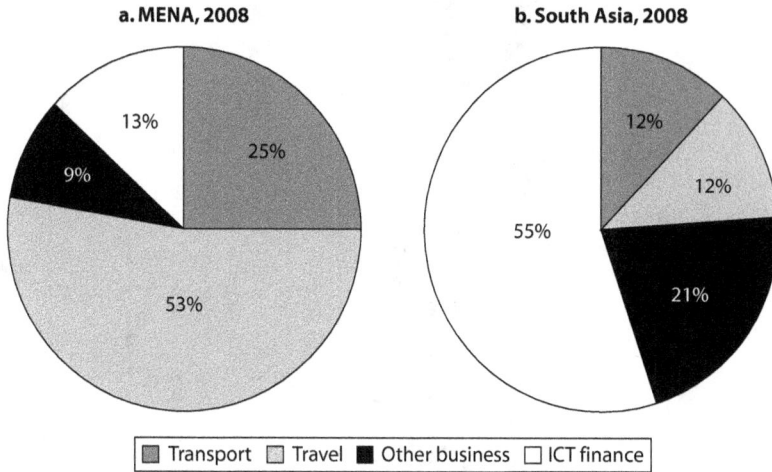

Transport ▨   Travel ▢   Other business ■   ICT finance ▢

Source: International Monetary Fund 2012.

of total MENA service exports. This contrasts sharply with South Asia, driven by India, where information and communications technology and finance are the leading export services, making up 55 percent of service exports. Transport and travel services account for only 24 percent of total service exports in that region (figure 3.2).

A significant portion of the services trade operates via temporary movements of people. While most MENA countries are labor exporters, labor demand from the Gulf Cooperation Council (GCC)—and especially from Saudi Arabia—is so high that the region is a net importer of labor vis-à-vis the rest of the world (table 3.1). The share of remittances inflows in GDP is especially high for labor-exporting countries like Lebanon, Jordan, Morocco, and Tunisia. Outflows of remittances are largest in the GCC, Lebanon, and the Syrian Arab Republic. More than 75 percent of the remittances flowing to the Arab Republic of Egypt, Jordan, and the West Bank and Gaza are from Arab countries, as compared to less than 15 percent for Algeria, Tunisia, and Morocco—countries that are more closely integrated with Europe.

The MENA region is a significant net importer of labor despite high unemployment rates. There are two main reasons for this apparent paradox. First, labor markets are not integrated at the regional level, despite significant bilateral flows between some countries. Second, labor-importing countries import mainly lower-skilled workers from Asia.

Table 3.1 Net Remittance Flows (current US$ millions)

Country	2000	2001	2002	2003	2004	2005	2006	2007	2008	2009
Net exporter of labor										
Algeria	790	670	1,070	1,750	2,460	2,060	1,610	2,120	2,202	2,059
Egypt, Arab Rep.	2,820	2,877	2,879	2,882	3,328	4,960	5,195	7,476	8,453	6,895
Jordan	1,648	1,818	1,949	1,974	2,058	2,150	2,482	2,955	3,322	3,095
Lebanon	1,582	2,307	24	662	1,359	913	1,757	2,807	2,815	1,809
Morocco	2,132	3,225	2,841	3,570	4,179	4,550	5,411	6,679	6,838	6,209
Syrian Arab Republic	151	140	100	849	813	783	560	899	1,188	1,120
Tunisia	769	906	1,057	1,233	1,418	1,377	1,494	1,701	1,961	1,952
West Bank and Gaza	1,004	1,061	1,030	550	625	698	920	1,076	1,210	1,251
Yemen, Rep.	1,227	1,231	1,230	1,210	1,174	1,173	1,162	1,003	1,074	823
Net importer of labor										
Bahrain	−1,013	−1,287	−872	−1,082	−1,120	−1,223	−1,531	−1,483	−1,774	−1,391
Kuwait	−1,734	−1,785	−1,926	−2,144	−2,404	−2,648	−3,183	−9,764	−10,323	−9,912
Libya	−454	−673	−779	−668	−965	−899	−929	−746	−948	−1,347
Oman	−1,412	−1,493	−1,563	−1,633	−1,787	−2,218	−2,749	−3,631	−5,142	−5,274
Saudi Arabia	15,390	−15,120	−15,854	−14,783	−13,555	−14,221	−15,858	−16,323	−21,480	−25,752
Iraq	—	—	—	—	—	629	−392	−14	40	−31
MENA	−10,183	−7,967	−10,308	−6,498	−2,857	−2,218	−4,397	−5,869	−11,569	19,448

Source: Staff calculations using the World Development Indicators dataset.

Note: Net remittance flows are computed as follows: remittances received − remittances paid; — = negligible.

By contrast, the region's labor exporters face stiff competition from the rest of the world, including developed countries, for workers at the high end of the skill spectrum. Although white-collar workers within the GCC do enjoy preferential access to labor markets in that subregion, the number of skilled workers in the GCC remains limited.

Impediments to the Services Trade

There are many impediments to trade services development. They include overvaluation of exchange rate, overregulation, and labor restrictions.

Dutch Disease Effects Reduce Competitive Services Production

The revolutions in technology and transportability that have occurred over the last 20 years have significantly changed the tradability of services and led to significant cross-border "disembodied" trade in services (Francois and Hoekman 2010). A large number of services sectors have become tradable. De Melo and Ugarte (forthcoming) show that, except for Iran and the Republic of Yemen, the real exchange rates of resource-rich economies in MENA were overvalued most of the time between 1980 and 2010, leading to an underdeveloped manufacturing sector (via the Dutch disease phenomenon).[1]

Using econometric analysis, Diop and De Melo (forthcoming) find that an overvalued exchange rate depresses services sector production in the region, especially in resource-rich countries. They show that demand for services has been booming in the region (owing to oil wealth and Engel's Law, which holds that, as income rises, the proportion of income spent on food falls, even if actual expenditure on food rises), but that much of this demand has been satisfied by imports, as domestic production of tradable services has been constrained by overvalued real exchange rates and Dutch disease effects. As a result, the share of services in GDP decreases with income in MENA's resource-rich countries, contrary to global trends. It appears from Diop and De Melo's econometric analysis that rents associated with natural resource abundance partially explain the negative correlation between services production and per-capita income.

Overregulation Stifles Investment and Trade in Services

Regulatory barriers to market entry, licensing, and business conduct remain significant in MENA compared to other regions. This situation is further complicated by the fact that countries have taken very different approaches to international services liberalization in the past, as illustrated by the diverse extent of General Agreement on Trade in Services (GATS) liberalization commitments among the region's World Trade Organization (WTO) members. In many instances, the extent of commitments reflects the status quo or even less than the prevailing situation, especially for members of the WTO's precursor, the General Agreement on Tariffs and Trade (GATT). These commitments have been assessed to be relatively modest and include several restrictions on the participation of foreigners. While regional service liberalization has begun in some countries (including Morocco, Jordan, and to some extent new WTO-acceding countries), the process lags behind in the region as a whole.

Recent analytical work sheds light on MENA countries' restrictiveness in five key services sectors as compared to the rest of the world. Borchert, Demartino, and Mattoo (2010) draw on a World Bank database of restrictions to trade in 11 Pan Arab Free Trade Agreement (PAFTA) countries (including the five GCC countries as well as Egypt, Jordan, Lebanon, Morocco, Tunisia, and the Republic of Yemen). This study finds that trade in financial services appears noticeably more restricted in MENA than in other countries at comparable income levels. In retail services, one of the most open sectors in the rest of the world, a number of restrictions persist in MENA countries. In telecommunications, most countries in the region have introduced at least some competition measures in both mobile and fixed-line services, so that the level of restrictions is similar to the rest of the world. Maritime transport is generally open, and progress has been made in cross-border air transport services; however, the protection afforded to national airlines and port services providers remains high. Finally, restrictions on access to professional services are widespread.

These findings are consistent with case studies conducted by the World Bank and others (box 3.1). Borchert, Demartino, and Mattoo (2010) identified the "desire on the part of government authorities to retain a considerable degree of regulatory discretion" as a distinctive feature of policies applied by PAFTA countries. As a result, even in areas free of explicit restrictions, *de jure* openness may not always imply a commensurate degree of *de facto* openness and vice-versa. In many instances, restrictions relate to business conduct or foreign equity limits. Across sectors, the granting of new licenses remains opaque and highly discretionary in many countries. This discretion leaves the rules of the game uncertain and may discourage domestic and foreign investors in the services sectors.

Box 3.1

Case Studies on Services Sector Liberalization

Case studies conducted in Morocco, Tunisia, Egypt, Jordan, and Lebanon show that services sectors in the region are liberalized, but only to a limited extent. Governments tend to retain control, leading to a lack of transparency and excessive discretion in how restrictions are applied.

In *banking*, Morocco and Tunisia display many restrictions. In particular, these countries' capital accounts are only partially open, leading to significant constraints to trade in services.

In *insurance*, Egypt is among the least restrictive countries in non-GCC MENA, reflecting the recent liberalization of the sector. However, specific restrictions on commercial presence and an Economic Needs Test requirement are noted. On the other end of the spectrum, Morocco and Tunisia have among the most restrictive regulatory environments, due mainly to restrictions on cross-border trade and consumption abroad. For Morocco, important nondiscriminatory concessions have been included as part of its free trade agreement with the United States (signed in 2004); once effective, the provisions in that agreement will open the sector significantly.

In *telecommunications*, Dihel and Shepherd (2007) note that countries of the Middle East rank among the most restrictive for entry in fixed telecommunications services (relative to Asian and transition economies). The sector is becoming more open in line with recent reforms, especially for mobile services. Morocco and Jordan have the most open telecommunications sectors in the region.

In *maritime transport*, major restrictions exist in Morocco and, to a lesser degree, in Egypt. In contrast, Tunisia and Jordan have fairly open maritime sectors. Across MENA countries, it is common to award preferential treatment to ships flying the national flag. Jordanian and Egyptian flag carriers, for instance, are given discounts on services such as port services. Egypt also gives flag carriers priority access to the cabotage market. In Morocco, regular shipping line services established in the country must fly the national flag. While open to foreign carriers, nonliner shipping is also restricted. Foreign shippers need to contract Moroccan liner intermediaries who have exclusivity in chartering foreign vessels.

In *air transport*, Egypt is highly restricted, and Jordan has the most open sector overall.

(continued next page)

Box 3.1 *(continued)*

Although foreign equity limits have been relaxed in most MENA countries in recent years, many service markets remain dominated by state-owned or domestic enterprises. High levels of state control persist in such cases through conflicting regulations that protect current market structures.

Sources: Dihel and Shepherd 2007 on telecommunications in the region; Marouani and Munro 2009 on Jordan, Egypt, and Lebanon; World Bank 2007a on Morocco; and World Bank 2007b on Tunisia.

Figure 3.3   Restrictiveness of Services Trade Policies and Share of Services in GDP, GCC, and Other Regions

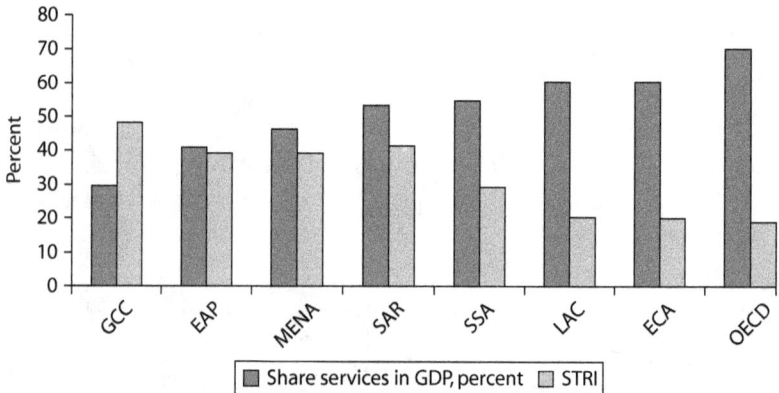

Source: Borchert, Gootiiz, and Mattoo 2012.

According to the Services Trade Restrictiveness Indices (STRI) calculated by Borchert, Demartino, and Mattoo (2010) using World Bank data on 102 countries, the GCC stands out as consistently more restrictive than other regions in the five sectors surveyed (figure 3.3). There appears to be a clear negative correlation between the magnitude of restrictions to trade in services and the share of services in GDP. The countries with the most open services sectors are those where services contribute the most to overall GDP.

Improving the delivery of core logistics services is an important factor in integrating global supply chains. Efficient trade logistics systems help support trade diversification and attract foreign direct investment (FDI). With the exception of the GCC and more recently the Maghreb, however, the MENA region's logistics performance has been weak, especially in Djibouti and the Republic of Yemen (figure 3.4).

Figure 3.4   Logistics Performance among Arab World Subregions

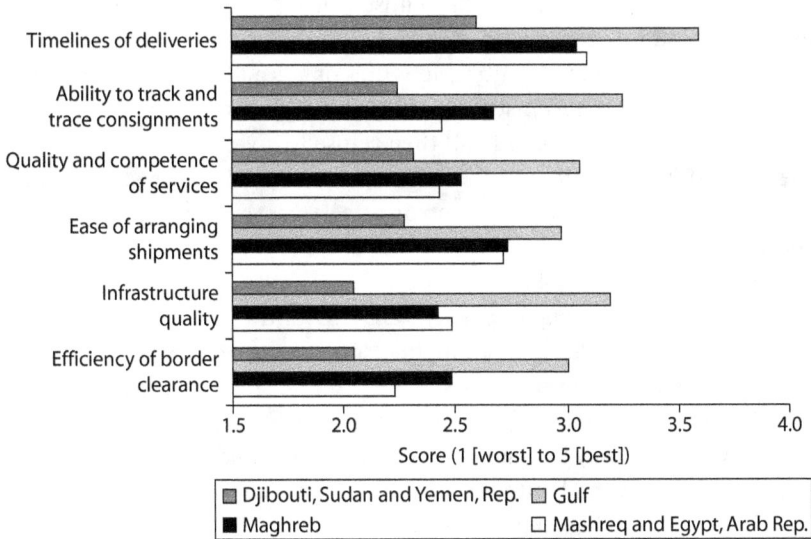

Source: Logistics Performance Index 2012.

Obstacles to the Movement of Labor

The movement of labor is constrained in the MENA region, largely as a result of labor market laws in MENA countries. These laws rarely distinguish between temporary and permanent labor mobility. Restrictions include burdensome and costly procedures for obtaining work permits, limitations on the length of stay, quantitative limits and sectoral bans on work permits, job nationalization, workers' educational status, restrictions on foreign investment, and restrictions on the mobility of family members.

Work permit procedures. Citizens of any GCC country are exempted from visa and work permit requirements when obtaining a job in another GCC country (Article 8, Chapter 2, GCC Agreement). However, an elaborate administrative mechanism exists to regulate the inflow of non-GCC migrant workers in GCC countries. All migrant workers and their dependents entering a GCC country are issued a resident visa for the number of years stipulated in the work contract. All such visas are issued under the authority of a sponsor (*kafil*) who wishes to hire the foreign worker. This rule applies to those hired to work in both the public and private sectors. Sponsorship is a necessary condition for recruiting foreign workers and is clearly stipulated in each country's domestic labor law.

Employers may either contact and recruit non-GCC workers directly after obtaining a permit from the Ministry of Labor or instruct a recruiting agent to supply them with foreign workers. Recruiting agents are not permitted to engage in recruiting activities unless a license is obtained for this purpose from the Ministry. In addition, employers are not allowed to bring in workers from abroad and then refuse to give them work or allow them to work for a third party.[2] The issuance, renewal, or transfer of work permits is subject to the payment of a fee that varies from country to country.

Limitations on the length of stay. GCC countries have similar labor policies regarding foreigners, though each country determines a specific duration of stay for foreign workers. In Bahrain, for example, residence permits under personal sponsorship are granted for a period not exceeding five years and may be renewed for a similar or shorter period, depending on the case. In the United Arab Emirates, the Labor Law allows work permits to be issued for a period of three years, but immigration authorities may issue them for a shorter period subject to a one-year minimum. In Kuwait, foreigners are allowed to work in the country for a maximum of three years, which may be renewable. In Qatar, the validity of a work permit is limited to the permitted residence period, so it may not exceed five years unless an exception is granted (Article 23, Law of 2004). Length of stay restrictions are much more stringent in the Maghreb. In Algeria, for example, temporary work permits are issued to foreign workers for a period not exceeding 3 months and cannot be renewed more than once a year. Algeria's Labor Law also stipulates that work permits should not exceed two years, though they may be renewable.

Job reservation. The labor laws of MENA countries grant employment priority to citizens when they are available and possess the capacity and competence to undertake the particular categories of employment offered. Countries usually impose quotas on the number of foreign workers at the national or sectoral level and sometimes apply specific quotas by firm. Furthermore, when the available labor force exceeds requirements, employers are required to release foreigners before citizens, provided that those citizens possess the required competence. In Bahrain and Qatar, labor laws state that when nationals do not have the required skills, they are to be trained by foreigners. These measures combine to deter trade in services, particularly when such trade requires cross-border movement of skilled personnel. In GCC countries, employment priority is granted to citizens, then to other GCC nationals, then to other Arab nationals and non-Arab nationals, respectively. When there is a surplus of workers, employers are to release workers in reverse order, provided that citizens or GCC nationals possess the competence required for employment. The labor laws of GCC countries also impose limits on the ratio of foreign to national workers. Under the Oman Labor Law of 2003 any employer who does not comply with the prescribed percentage of "Omanisation" will be fined a sum equal to 50 percent of the average total salary among non-Omani employees.

Regulated professions. Agreements on the mutual recognition of diplomas concerning regulated professions are rare in the MENA region. Regulated professions are not always clearly specified in countries' labor laws; as a result, only a few relevant examples are presented here. Egyptian law clearly states that any doctor working in an Egyptian health center should be Egyptian.[3] To be allowed to work in Egyptian health centers, non-Egyptians must be registered with the Medical Association and deemed experts in a field in which there is a lack of Egyptian specialists. A special permit from the Minister of Health and the Medical Association is also required. Similar regulations govern the areas of veterinary medicine, pharmacy, and dentistry. Non-Egyptians are not allowed to work as lawyers, with few exceptions.[4] In Jordan, certain categories of employment are reserved for nationals, including in public and governmental sectors, in areas such as law and accounting, and in occupations related to national security or defense. In Libya, positions as accountants, typists, drivers, and guards are reserved for Libyan nationals (Otman and Karlberg 2007). By contrast, the United Arab Emirates has opened some previously regulated professions (in the fields of medicine, the law, accounting and auditing, and engineering, as well as managerial, economic, technical, agricultural, fishing, and industrial consultation positions) to practitioners and employees of any nationality of the states of the Arab Cooperation Council (ACC).[5]

Regional Trade Agreements and Service Flows

Most of the economic agreements signed in the MENA region at the bilateral, regional, and international levels have aimed to liberalize the trade of goods and commodities. Little attention has been accorded to the liberalization of services, however.

Bilateral agreements have been the main vehicle for fostering trade in services among neighboring countries. Lebanon has initiated several such bilateral agreements, including one with Iraq that aims to strengthen economic cooperation. Article 3 of the agreement between Lebanon and Iraq mentions that the parties should exchange expertise, specialists, and trainers. Similarly, Lebanon and Kuwait have reached an agreement in which it is mentioned that the two parties shall facilitate the procedure of granting entry visas to businessmen in both countries (Article 6). Lebanon and Syria have agreed to promote labor mobility between their countries. However, even if these agreements include some provisions related to exchanging expertise or facilitating visa procedures, they do not include direct provisions for organizing the temporary movement of workers.

One of the most successful bilateral agreements in the region is that between Egypt and Jordan, which was signed in 1985 with the aim of facilitating labor migration between the two countries. The agreement stipulates that Egyptian workers will have the same rights as Jordanian workers with regard to the labor law, social benefits, and insurance. Yet the agreement was amended in 2007, reducing the duration of the contract between employee and employer from two years to one year. In addition, no worker is allowed to change employment prior to the end of his or her contract without involving the Ministries of Manpower in both countries. Over the past few years, the agreement has succeeded in increasing the number of Egyptian workers employed in various fields and sectors in Jordan. Two-thirds of all work permits issued to foreign workers in Jordan have been given to Egyptians, primarily in the agricultural sector (34 percent), manufacturing and commercial activities (17 percent), and the services sector (12 percent).

Conclusion

Unleashing the potential of the services sectors in MENA will require implementing key macro- and microeconomic reforms. On the macro front, avoiding significant overvaluation of real exchange rates will be crucial in resource-rich countries, where rents from natural resources undermine development of the sector. In all countries, decisive microeconomic reforms are needed to remove barriers to entry and business conduct and to enhance domestic and international competition in services. Finally, reducing obstacles to regional labor movement through trade agreements and mutual recognition of diplomas would help to improve labor resource allocation and maximize regional growth. Addressing these issues would have a direct impact on employment, the overriding problem of MENA countries, as services sectors are labor-intensive and thus critical for reducing unemployment.

MENA countries have much to gain from regional services liberalization. Comprehensive reforms to strengthen competition and streamline regulatory frameworks would yield benefits two to three times greater than those achieved through tariff removal alone (Konan 2003). In particular, opening the services trade in the region would facilitate trade in parts and components and contribute to the emergence of regional production networks.

Notes

1. An increase in revenues from oil exports will make the country's currency stronger compared to that of other nations, resulting in the country's other exports becoming more expensive for other countries to buy, thus making the manufacturing sector less competitive.

2. In addition to sponsorship, the following conditions are often required to obtain work permits in GCC countries: (i) a medical test; (ii) proof of academic qualifications (Kuwait, Oman); or (iii) a minimum bank deposit (Bahrain).

3. Article 8 of Law 51/1981 on the regulation of medical institutions.

4. Exceptions are made for Palestinians and Sudanese citizens, and for citizens of Arab States that signed agreements with Egypt stipulating the right of Egyptian lawyers to join their Bar Associations. Law 17/1983.

5. Federal Law No. (2), year 1984.

References

Borchert, Ingo, Samantha Demartino, and Aaditya Mattoo. 2010. *Services Trade Policies in the Pan-Arab Free Trade Area (PAFTA)*. Draft report, Trade and Integration Team of the Development Research Group (DECTI), World Bank, Washington, DC.

Borchert, Ingo, Batshur Gootiiz, and Aaditya Mattoo. 2012. "Policy Barriers to International Trade in Services: Evidence from a New Database." Policy Research Working Paper 6109, World Bank, Washington, DC.

De Melo, Jaime, and Cristian Ugarte. Forthcoming. "Resource Abundance and Growth Performance: Benchmarking MENA." In *Natural Resource Abundance, Growth, and Diversification in the Middle East and North Africa: The Effects on Natural Resources and the Role of Policies*, ed. Ndiamé Diop, Daniela Marotta, and Jaime De Melo. Directions in Development. Washington, DC: World Bank.

Dihel, Nora, and Ben Shepherd. 2007. "Modal Estimates of Services Barriers." OECD Trade Policy Working Papers No. 51, OECD Publishing, Paris.

Diop, Ndiamé, and Jaime De Melo. Forthcoming. "Rents, Regulatory Restrictions, and Diversification towards Services in Resource-Rich MENA." In *Natural Resource Abundance, Growth, and Diversification in the Middle East and North Africa: The Effects on Natural Resources and the Role of Policies*, ed. Ndiamé Diop, Daniela Marotta, and Jaime De Melo. Directions in Development series. Washington, DC: World Bank.

Francois, Joseph, and Bernard Hoekman. 2010. "Services Trade and Policy." *Journal of Economic Literature* 48 (3): 642–92.

International Monetary Fund. 2012. *Direction of Trade*. Washington, DC: International Monetary Fund.

Konan, Denise E. 2003. "Alternative Paths to Prosperity: Trade Liberalization in Egypt and Tunisia." In *Arab Economic Integration: Between Hope and Reality*, ed. Ahmed Galal and Bernard Hoekman. Washington, DC: Brookings Institution Press.

Logistics Performance Index. 2012. World Bank, Washington, DC.

Marouani, Mohamed Ali, and Laura Munro. 2009. "Assessing Barriers to Trade in Services in the MENA Region." OECD Trade Policy Working Paper No. 84. OECD Publishing, Paris.

Otman, Waniss A., and Erling Karlberg. 2007. "The Libyan Legal System and Key Recent Legislation." In *The Libyan Economy: Economic Diversification and International Repositioning*, ed. Waniss A. Otman and Erling Karlberg, 63–86. New York: Springer.

World Bank. 2007a. "Morocco's Backbone Services Sectors: Reforms for Higher Productivity and Deeper Integration with Europe." Draft Report No. 39755-MA, World Bank, Washington, DC.

———. 2007b. "Tunisia's Global Integration: Second Generation of Reforms to Boost Growth and Employment." Draft Report No. 40129-TN, World Bank, Washington, DC.

World Development Indicators. 2012. World Bank, Washington, DC.

CHAPTER 4

Cross-Border Infrastructure: Building Backbone Services

Ensuring that backbone services such as telecommunications, transport, and power are widely accessible, of good quality, and delivered efficiently is critical to boosting productivity and international competitiveness. Backbone services are major determinants of production costs. Opening these services to competition, encouraging trade, and harmonizing sector regulations can help reduce production costs, increase foreign direct investment (FDI), promote knowledge spillovers, and expand markets. Wider regional infrastructure networks can bring economies of scale and scope that reduce costs and improve service quality. Boosting competitiveness through better backbone services will ultimately result in higher employment, growth, and improved living standards.

The Transport Sector—Extensive but Often Deficient Networks

For most Middle East and North Africa (MENA) countries, the transport sector is key to regional economic integration. Most MENA countries have extensive road networks, with high capacity in some areas, as well as important facilities for air and sea transport, and, in several instances, a sizable rail network. However, the quality of transport infrastructure is often deficient and unable to support growing, modern economies. Even where road networks are in place, trucking services tend to be unsatisfactory due to the continued use of outdated vehicles, excess capacity, and weaknesses in the structure of the road freight industry. Some potentially important trade corridors are hampered by the absence of road links between Algeria and Morocco; railway links and standardization between Algeria, Morocco, and Tunisia; and highway links between Libya and Tunisia. Performance of the port sector, which is the main determinant of trade costs between countries, hinges on the extent to which countries develop and rely on regional hubs and make use of efficient port concessionaires.

Ports and Railways

Trade among MENA countries is limited. Trade flows with the European Union (EU), United States, and China are far more significant. Of primary concern, therefore, is the efficiency of existing trade corridors connecting MENA countries with these major global markets. Data on typical distance, lead time, and cost per 20-foot container (TEU) traveling via a port and maritime corridor suggest that lead times for import and export are fairly modest, but that the cost of trading one ton across a border varies by a factor of 10 across countries in the region (table 4.1).

Table 4.1   Time and Cost Data for MENA Import and Export Container Movements

	Export			Import		
	Distance (km)	Lead time (days)	Cost ($)	Distance (km)	Lead time (days)	Cost ($)
Morocco	247	3	500	247	3	500
Algeria	75	8	1,000	750	39	2,000
Tunisia	300	2	250	300	1	250
Libya	43	2	548	25	4	671
Egypt, Arab Rep.	280	2	773	346	3	1,123
Israel	115	2	487	81	2	595
Lebanon	60	2	672	82	3	975
Syrian Arab Republic	300	3	866	300	4	1,225
Jordan	300	3	572	300	5	1,000
Saudi Arabia	132	5	506	145	6	1,225
United Arab Emirates	166	1	495	103	2	618

Source: Logistics Performance Index 2012.
Note: It seems that "distance" and "lead time" were interpreted by most survey respondents as referring to transport between the main city (or cities) and the nearest port, whereas the cost refers to the transport to/from the external market.

Costs are particularly high in Algeria, the Arab Republic of Egypt, and the Syrian Arab Republic, and far lower in Tunisia and Morocco.

Many of the world's busiest shipping lines pass through the heart of the MENA region, so connectivity is rarely an issue. Scheduled sailings of ships carrying containers are frequent,[1] from the Straits of Gibraltar to the Suez Canal, then through the Red Sea and eastward into the Indian Ocean. The ports of Syria and Lebanon are not served directly by shipping lines plying between Europe and the Far East, but they handle substantial volumes of traffic from Europe to third countries—notably Saudi Arabia and other Gulf Cooperation Council (GCC) countries—thus enjoying the economies of scale and frequency offered by a busy port. Only two countries in the region, Jordan and Iraq, enjoy no such advantage, as each has only one seaport (Aqaba and Umm Qasr, respectively) and both are somewhat removed from more heavily traded routes.

Container costs vary widely in MENA, as mentioned above. These costs are a function of service frequency, economies of scale in ships and ports, and the extent to which discounts are available in the backhaul direction. By analyzing these factors in combination, stakeholders can determine whether there will be enough traffic to justify direct services from origin to destination without transshipment on the way, which adds costs and lengthens trip times.

Given the significant savings that can be gained by concentrating traffic on a few large ships rather than many smaller ones, developing and making use of hub ports is vital to trading competitively across borders. The choice is often between direct services from A to B with medium-sized ships and medium frequency, or indirect services via a hub that allows greater frequency and, thanks to the consolidation of loads, larger ships that lower unit transport costs for the maritime leg, offset to some extent by the costs of transshipment (typically US$ 100–120 per lift per TEU) at the hub. Countries served directly by a hub port therefore enjoy a considerable advantage over those that must rely on feeder services via a hub in a third country.

The MENA region is home to several shipping hubs, with varying levels of direct service. The notable hub ports of the Mediterranean are Tanger-Med in Morocco and the two Egyptian ports: Port Said at the Mediterranean end of the Suez Canal, and Damietta to the west of the canal entrance. Serving the Gulf states on the Suez Canal-India maritime corridor, the biggest hub ports are Jeddah, Saudi Arabia, in the Red Sea, and Salalah, Oman, in the Indian Ocean/Arabian Sea. There are several hubs in the Persian Gulf itself: Dubai and Abu Dhabi serving the

United Arab Emirates, Doha serving Qatar, Dammam serving Saudi Arabia, and Bandar Abbas serving the Islamic Republic of Iran. These hubs bestow on their home economies the savings of direct service by the world's largest container ships and car carriers from New York, northwestern Europe, Singapore, and China. By contrast, for longer voyages smaller ports like Umm Qasr must rely on feeder ships via the nearest hub or shoulder the higher costs and lower frequencies of direct lines.

Several countries in the eastern Mediterranean have declared their intention to invest heavily to develop their national ports into international hubs, but they will face stiff competition from existing international hubs. Moreover, the global economic crisis that began in 2008 has forced many of these ambitious plans to be scaled back until confidence in renewed trade growth is restored.

Another critical factor in gaining a competitive edge in shipping is the competence of a port's concessionnaire. Management of most of the hub ports in the Mediterranean and the Gulf is now concessioned out to one or the other of the world's largest and most experienced port operators. As a result, an important share of shipping costs depends on the entrepreneurial skills of the concessionaire and the extent of its global network, on which it can draw to optimize ship routing and scheduling and minimize ocean freight rates, consistent with reasonably frequent and predictable deliveries.

The distance between ports of the eastern Mediterranean and those of the Gulf states are significant, prompting questions about whether rail transport might be less costly. For example, the distance between Lattakia, Syria, and Baghdad, Iraq, is 1,000 km. The distance between Beirut, Lebanon, or Tartous, Syria, to Riyadh, Saudi Arabia, is 2,000 km. Services between Lattakia and Baghdad have been disrupted for many years by the war in Iraq and are only now being restored. No rail link currently connects Saudi Arabia with the Mediterranean, but the Kingdom is planning to build a rail line from Riyadh to the Jordanian border near Amman (about 1,400 km) and has announced a railway linking its bauxite and phosphorus mines in the far north with planned Gulf coast processing and export facilities at Ras Al-Zour on the Gulf (about 2,400 km), connecting from there to the GCC railway. It will be many years, however, before imports will be able to go by rail from one of the Syrian ports via Amman to the Gulf cities.

There is limited precedent in the MENA region for railways, whether old or new, that are managed well enough to compete successfully with trucking. In the entire region, only the Iranian and Moroccan railways

perform reasonably well in carrying general freight. The railways of
Tunisia and Jordan serve their respective phosphate export flows quite
well, but at a financial loss, which impedes them from investing in service
improvements. The only railways to make a profit (even after subsidies)
have been in the Islamic Republic of Iran, Morocco, and Syria. Egypt was
the biggest loser, proportionally, with operating costs (including deprecia-
tion) exceeding revenues (including subsidies) by almost 50 percent. This
was the result of the Egyptian government's policy of operating dense
passenger services at low fares; passenger traffic comprised more than
90 percent of total operations.

Issues in Intraregional Transport

Morocco-Algeria. Transport flows between Morocco and Algeria are fun-
damentally impeded by the closed border between the two countries.
Triggered by a security incident, the border was closed to road and rail
traffic in 1994 and prevents, by extension, overland travel between
Morocco and Tunisia. Algeria, however, has nearly completed construction of its East-West Motorway (1,216 km), which runs from its border
with Tunisia (in the corridor serving Tunis and its environs) to Tlemcen
near its western border, and opposite Oujda, the border town on the
Moroccan side. Morocco and Tunisia are in the process of completing
comparably high-standard highways on their respective sides of the border, aligned and with technical standards that are compatible with the
Algerian motorway. At a technical level, the ministries of public works of
Morocco and Algeria have cooperated to ensure continuity at the border
when the political will materializes to reopen it. Similarly, the railway
companies of the two countries have coordinated plans for a future high-
speed passenger line to link Tangiers, Casablanca, and Rabat in Morocco
with Algiers and Tunis.

Tunisia-Libya. In Libya, under the Ghaddafi regime, plans were prepared
for the construction of a coastal motorway from the Tunisian border to
the Egyptian border, a distance of 1,700 km. The Italian government had
expressed interest in financing it, but no start has been made. There are
also plans for the construction of a railway line from the Tunisian border
to the Egyptian border (2,178 km, including feeder lines). It was designed
to carry freight using standard-gauge track, as is found in Egypt and in the
Maghreb lines other than those south of Tunis, which are narrow gauge
(1 meter). Chinese and Russian state financing was secured and contrac-
tors from these countries were engaged. Earthworks are underway

between the Tunisian border and Tripoli. However, the Chinese work-force was repatriated during the recent period of armed conflict in Libya, and some time may be required before work resumes.

The Tunisian government is considering alternatives for dealing with the difference in railway gauges. One option is to build the "missing link" within Tunisia from the Libyan border to Gabes (200 km) to standard gauge and to add a single track of standard gauge between Gabes and Tunis (about 400 km), alongside the existing narrow-gauge tracks, to provide continuity between Tripoli and Tunis. At US$ 0.5–0.7 million per km, the construction cost of this endeavor would amount to about US$ 300–400 million, which would be justified only if traffic is likely to exceed 1.0–1.5 million tons per year.

Egypt-Jordan-Saudi Arabia. The current extension of the highway and railway along the Egyptian coast is broadly adequate for foreseeable traffic volumes, at least for the desert portion as far as Alexandria. Along the Nile Delta, on the other hand, population density is higher, space is at a premium, and many main roads are underdesigned and severely congested.

Currently, road traffic between Egypt and Jordan, and by extension to Saudi Arabia and the Gulf, must take a ferry from the Egyptian town of Nuweiba on the Gulf of Aqaba to the port of Aqaba. The ferry trip is short (about 50 km), but it adds considerably to total trip time. Complaints have been heard that, on occasion, truck traffic has exceeded ferry capacity by such a degree that perishable cargoes have spoiled while waiting in line for days before the next available sailing. This bottleneck would be eliminated if Egypt could reach agreement with Israel to allow such traffic to transit 15 km through Israel's extreme southern tip, at Eilat, to reach Aqaba without the need for a ferry.

The Mashreq: Syria, Lebanon, Israel, Jordan, and Iraq. Door-to-door shipping delivery from cities in the Mashreq subregion take at least 1 week, even to the closest international destinations, and about 1 month for the longer routes to Asia. The seven Mashreq ports (Lattakia and Tartous, in Syria; Beirut and Tripoli, in Lebanon; Haifa, in Israel; Aqaba, in Jordan; and Umm Qasr, in Iraq) have experienced strong growth in container traffic and a significant increase in productivity during the last decade. They all remain of medium size, however, each handling less than 1 million TEU per year. With the exception of Umm Qasr, they have facilities and draft able to accommodate vessels up to about 4,000 TEU (the Panama Canal limit). They serve as feeder ports but attract few direct services. Only in Beirut are volumes of transshipped containers significant. Beirut and Lattakia are being expanded with new berths, but it remains to be seen whether either port can capture the role of hub port for the eastern Mediterranean, in competition with Mersin, in Turkey, and others.

Saudi Arabia. Changes underway in Saudi Arabia will benefit freight movements. The Dammam-Riyadh railway is to be extended to the Jordanian border, and various plans have been drawn up to connect the Gulf states by rail.[2]

Iran-Turkey corridor. For decades, the Islamic Republic of Iran has examined options for shortening the time and lowering the cost of land transport between Tehran and its relatively densely populated northwestern region, on the one hand, and central Turkey on the other. The distances are long (2,300 km from Ankara to Tehran), through rugged terrain. Road transport has served high-value trade between the countries of Eastern Europe and western Asia (mostly imports to the Islamic Republic of Iran) well enough in general, while low-value trade has preferred maritime transport. More recently, the Islamic Republic of Iran has invested heavily in expanding the capacity of its two Indian Ocean ports: Bandar Abbas at the "neck" of the Gulf, and Chahbahar near the border with Pakistan. These ports also serve trade with southern and eastern Asia.

The attraction of rail service between Istanbul/Ankara and Tehran would grow considerably if Turkey were to undertake one key infrastructure investment. Lake Van, in southeastern Turkey, still requires a railway ferry from one end of the lake to the other, owing to the difficult terrain around the lake's edge. Construction of the missing rail link along the shore would be costly but would cut travel time by several hours. As recently as 2008, serious negotiations have been conducted with a view to launching construction of the missing link.

Improving Regional Transport Policies
Reforming trucking. Throughout much of the MENA region, trucking is atomized and provides poor-quality service locally. International trucking tends to be a distinct sector, operated by large fleets with modern tractor-trailers. Yet competition from the low end of the market erodes the profitability of "modern" trucking firms. Jordan recently eliminated the traditional queuing approach for trucks waiting to pick up cargo at the port of Aqaba, replacing it with a system that requires each truck

to enter into a contract before going to the port. This change has radically improved the utilization of trucks and eliminated the congestion previously caused by large numbers of idling trucks waiting their turn on the outskirts of Aqaba. Syria, by contrast, still operates under the traditional queuing approach.

Transit guarantees. Many of the trucks crossing one country to reach another are currently required by the relevant customs agency to travel in convoy with a police escort in order to ensure that goods subject to import duty in the transit country are not diverted into the local economy without the duty being paid. In addition to incurring substantial fees, the trucks in transit have to wait unpredictable amounts of time while the convoy is formed. This system is used particularly in the Mashreq and Gulf countries.

The TIR (Transports Internationaux Routiers) system of transit guarantees, if put in place, would greatly reduce the need for such convoys as well as the associated fees and delays. The TIR system is complex institutionally, but effective. It requires trucking firms in each country to form an association with the financial means to arrange bank guarantees for its members, and for the firms to meet professional standards set by the International Road Transport Union (IRU). Firms that comply are then allowed to use TIR carnets, at a low cost per trip, as a transit document accepted by customs authorities from origin to destination and guaranteed by the IRU, exempting the carriers from other, costlier forms of guarantee or transit in convoy.

Jordan does not recognize the TIR system, but has been experimenting recently with global positioning system (GPS)-backed tracking devices for trucks in transit. This is simpler institutionally, though concerns have been expressed about the feasibility of finding and seizing trucks that fail to adhere to the designated transit route.

Commercializing railways. Railways in the region have been managed as state enterprises, with minimal commercial discipline and incentives. The result is poor service quality, which has repelled large potential demand. The Islamic Republic of Iran, Morocco, and, to a lesser degree, Tunisia, are encouraging efficient railway management. The development of a modern rail network in Saudi Arabia and the rebuilding of railway operations in Iraq provide opportunities to introduce private sector participation, reorganize with a business-oriented focus, and create stronger commercial incentives for management.

Organizing ports on the landlord model. Most ports in the region are restructuring into or have already moved to a landlord model,[3] which has proved favorable when implemented in a transparent and accountable manner. Egypt still has something of a hybrid, as its public sector port companies blur the line between entities that provide port infrastructure and those that operate the terminals. The GCC is ahead of the curve with Dubai Ports World, which has become a world leader among transport hubs worldwide.

The Power Sector—Initiatives Underway to Interconnect Electricity Networks

Strong growth in electricity demand in the MENA region will require sizable investments in power sector infrastructure, possibly as high as US$ 450 billion over the next decade. Investment will also be needed in the primary fuels markets to develop and deliver the region's substantial gas reserves, which will fuel the new generating capacity. Fostering cross-border trade in the power sector could help alleviate supply constraints and reduce the investment required to meet the rapidly growing demand for power.

There are numerous obstacles to electricity trade in the region, including the tight generation demand/supply situation in most Arab countries and the absence of a harmonized regulatory framework with clear rules governing electricity trade. Though Arab countries hold about 30 percent of the world's proven gas reserves, every country in the region except Qatar and Algeria falls short of the gas supply needed to meet current and projected national demand. Increased energy (gas and electricity) integration and trade will therefore help improve the security and sustainability of the region's energy supplies. Solar energy holds tremendous potential, but cross-border investment may be needed to realize economies of scale and scope in this area.

Challenges to Power Sector Integration

The lack of infrastructure and development in the energy sector poses a significant barrier to increased trade and cooperation in the MENA region. Many MENA countries lack the reserve margin levels needed to ensure supply adequacy. Further exacerbating this situation is the limited amount of natural gas available to power-generating stations.

Recognizing the benefits of regional integration, several bilateral and subregional initiatives are underway to interconnect the electricity networks of MENA countries. The primary regional interconnection schemes among MENA countries include:

- The Maghreb regional interconnection, which includes Morocco, Algeria, and Tunisia. It was initiated in the 1950s and has evolved into multiple high-voltage transmission interconnections between the three countries. Morocco was connected to Spain in the late 1990s, and Morocco, Algeria, and Tunisia are now all synchronized with the pan-European high-voltage transmission network.

- The eight-country and territories interconnection (ECI), which includes Egypt, Iraq, Jordan, Lebanon, Libya, Syria and Turkey; together with the West Bank and Gaza. It was initiated in 1988 by Egypt, Iraq, Jordan, Syria, and Turkey as part of an effort to upgrade their electricity systems to a regional standard. Lebanon, Libya, and West Bank and Gaza later extended the agreement to eight countries. Turkey fully synchronized its grid with the European grid in 2011 and plans to start trading commercially soon.

- The regional power interconnection of the GCC allows electricity exchange among its six member states—Kuwait, Saudi Arabia, Bahrain, Qatar, the United Arab Emirates, and Oman—under an agreement signed in 2009. The interconnection is targeted at sharing capacity reserves and improving supply reliability, which will reduce the need for investment in new generation capacity.

Though the Maghreb and ECI interconnections have existed for some time, electricity trade among Arab countries has remained modest. Similarly, trade among GCC countries has been limited, owing to the emphasis on reserve sharing and reliability, and to the fact that the interconnection and associated agreements have only recently been put into place. Trade cannot currently take place between the GCC and other MENA countries, as there are no physical interconnections. This may change, as electrical interconnections between the United Arab Emirates and the Islamic Republic of Iran, and between Saudi Arabia and Egypt, are under consideration. Trade is also currently unworkable between the ECI and the Maghreb via the interconnection between Tunisia and Libya because the Maghreb and ECI systems are not synchronized.

The Mediterranean ring initiative is attempting to synchronize the electricity networks of all European and MENA countries bordering the

Mediterranean Sea.[4] In addition, Turkey is expected to join the EU electricity market in 2012. In the longer term, this would pave the way for the ECI countries, and potentially the GCC through the proposed Saudi Arabia-Egypt interconnection, to synchronize and join the EU market in the future.

Power demand is forecast to grow significantly in the MENA region at an average annual rate of about 6.4 percent. This rapid demand growth implies the need for over 150,000 MW of new generating capacity (68 percent of existing capacity) by 2020, not including the generation capacity needed to replace retired plants. The investment cost for new generating capacity could approach US$ 225 billion (assuming US$ 1,500/kW for new gas combined-cycle technology). When factoring in the transmission and distribution facilities necessary to meet the increased demand, the total investment cost for new infrastructure in the MENA region's power sector could top US$ 450 billion by 2020. Furthermore, if it is assumed that 70 percent of the new generating capacity will be fired with natural gas, costs for gas alone could exceed US$ 26 billion annually (assuming a 60 percent load factor, about 550 TWh annually would be produced from natural gas at US$ 48/MWh).[5] These costs could be greatly reduced, perhaps by as much as 10 percent, through a regional, rather than national, approach to the planning and operation of the power sector in MENA.

One important benefit of regional integration could stem from MENA's considerable wind and solar energy potential, estimated at 630,000,000 MW (630 TW) of solar power and 75,000 MW of wind power.[6] Unlike oil and gas, wind and solar energy are spread more evenly across MENA countries, presenting a unique opportunity for further regional integration to enhance economic growth and reduce poverty. For oil and gas importers, renewable energy would provide energy security; for oil and gas exporters, it would free up fossil fuels for higher value-added usage and exports. The prospect of exporting green energy to Europe at high prices enhances the likelihood that renewable energy could become an important and reliable source of revenue for MENA countries and, as envisioned in the Desertec concept, provide a sustainable supply of energy to Middle Eastern, North African, and European countries by 2050. The Desertec concept inspired the design of the Mediterranean Solar Plan, one of the six pillars of the Union for the Mediterranean, which aims to develop 20 GW of renewable energy (mainly solar), with 5 GW to be exported to Europe.

Despite the tremendous opportunities to increase electricity trade among MENA countries, there are many physical, structural, institutional, and regulatory challenges, as outlined below.

Physical Challenges
- High-voltage interconnecting transmission lines exist, but not all MENA countries are interconnected and not all systems are synchronized. While there is interconnection capacity available to increase trade, it is not large enough to support large-scale development of generation capacity.
- Because the electricity systems of some MENA countries have not been designed to meet minimum standards, there may be reliability and security risks associated with expanding interconnection capacity in the region. Only three countries—Algeria, Morocco, and Tunisia—are currently synchronized with the EU grid.
- The amount of surplus power available in MENA countries to support long-term trade is limited.

Structural and Institutional Challenges
- There is minimal coordinated control over many national networks, which makes it difficult to determine and verify whether international trade transactions are feasible. There are no control centers responsible for coordinating generation and transmission operations in the subregions, though the GCC Interconnection Authority has limited control over international transactions in the GCC.
- The electricity markets in most MENA countries remain vertically integrated, state-owned monopolies. There are no "eligible customers" with the opportunity to choose their supplier. As a result, international transactions take a long time to negotiate and are generally unable to respond to short-term opportunities such as sudden changes in generation availability.
- While there are some regional organizations in place, they are few, cover too few countries, and have limited duties and power to enforce their decisions.
- Only a few MENA countries have shown an interest in electricity market reform at the national level. As competition is limited, market monitoring and surveillance guidelines have not been established.
- Private sector participation in electricity markets is generally limited to independent power producers and independent water and power producers. By providing third-party access to the transmission grid and

regional trade, the private sector can help mobilize the large amounts of capital necessary to fund the projects that are needed to meet growing electricity demand.

- A number of MENA countries have high technical and commercial losses and poor collection rates, adding to the power companies' financial woes and creditworthiness issues.

Regulatory Challenges

- There is minimal harmonization of legislation among MENA countries with respect to energy, environment, and safety.
- Few MENA countries have what could be considered "independent and informed" regulatory agencies. Independence refers to the ability to make decisions in the absence of political interference. Informed means that the members of the regulatory agency have the background, expertise, and skills to make decisions on behalf of all participants in the power sector. Regulation should be the primary job of the staff of the regulatory agencies, which is often not the case in MENA countries.
- There is significant subsidization and cross-subsidization of pricing in the power sectors of MENA countries. Retail tariffs are generally well below the cost of supply and there is often cross-subsidization of tariffs by larger industrial customers on behalf of smaller households. It is difficult to find a creditworthy off-taker since many power companies are at or near bankruptcy. It also makes it difficult to find a buyer, as potential customers are paying prices for power that are well below cost. A potential customer is unlikely to buy power at international prices when power can be purchased in the domestic market at subsidized prices.
- Gas markets in MENA countries have generally not been deregulated. This poses a significant challenge to sustainability and environmental objectives and to the promotion of competition. Internationally, gas markets are often liberalized in tandem with electricity markets. The environmental advantages of gas make it the fossil fuel of choice for electricity generation. In MENA countries, both oil and gas prices used for electricity generation are often subsidized at levels well below international prices. As a result, fuel is being used inefficiently in the production process, and consumption is inefficient because retail electricity prices are well below the opportunity cost of supply. Furthermore, subsidized fuel prices complicate electricity pricing, as it is difficult to determine a fair price for both long- and short-term trades.

- Most MENA countries do not allow access to their transmission networks under published terms, conditions, and prices, such that access cannot be considered fair and nondiscriminatory.
- There is very little published information concerning market prices and transmission availability.
- MENA countries are characterized by an excessive diversity of accounting practices and an absence of secure and stable legal frameworks.

Power Sector Integration Agenda

To promote regional integration and trade in MENA's power sector, reforms will need to encourage fair and open access to national transmission systems. It will be important for reforms to be implemented to ensure reciprocity and a level playing field, governed by technical and financial documentation and high-level institutions with the expertise and authority to guide and, if necessary, enforce some degree of consistency and fairness across the region. An appropriate long-term goal would be to achieve a regional electricity market that allows all market participants, regardless of origin, fair and open access to the transmission system.[7]

An implementable regional market design that might serve as the first step in MENA's market reform process would include a number of steps. First, each country would be required to meet minimum reliability criteria as documented in a Regional Grid Code. Second, eligible regional market participants would be free to negotiate bilateral contracts for capacity or energy with any other eligible regional market participant. The technical feasibility of bilateral contracts would be confirmed in advance by the subregional transmission system operator (TSO) or market facilitator, who would in turn inform each national TSO that might be affected by the transaction. Third, fair and open access to each country's transmission networks would be provided at published terms, conditions, and prices, with transmission services harmonized across each subregional market. Fourth, transmission service tariffs would need to be sufficient to recover the cost of capital, operations and maintenance of transmission assets, and other ancillary services necessary to support bilateral transactions. It would be important for transmission tariffs to be calculated in a transparent and nondiscriminatory manner, and to be sufficient to cover network expansion. Fifth, a TSO/market facilitator would facilitate trade at the subregional level by publishing market prices for each country; these would be used to identify trade opportunities and would provide a reference price for use in freely negotiated bilateral contracts.

The proper functioning of a regional electricity market requires a clear set of market rules, or a commercial code, and a grid code. The market rules should cover commercial aspects of the regional market. These would identify the legal status and responsibilities of the regional market institutions and regional market participants; the services to be traded and procedures for trade; responsibilities and payment for transmission services, metering, billing, settlement, and payment guarantees; roles in planning and coordination; mechanisms for exchange and publication of market information; and administrative matters such as *force majeure*, confidentiality, liability, review and amendment procedures, dispute resolution mechanisms, and termination. The grid code legally establishes the technical requirements for the connection to, and use of, the transmission system by network users in a manner that ensures reliable, efficient, and safe operation. The grid code enables the TSO to manage the high-voltage transmission network in a safe, secure, and economical manner. It provides a level playing field for the nondiscriminatory and transparent use of the transmission network.

Numerous policy and institutional reforms could be pursued in the MENA region to increase regional integration and trade (box 4.1).

If regional integration and trade are to increase, infrastructure must be improved and expanded to increase capacity and synchronize the power grid. Necessary infrastructure improvements include reinforcing existing cross-border interconnections and upgrading national transmission networks, as well as constructing new international interconnections. Expanding generation capacity in certain countries for export to other market destinations, particularly renewable energy developments, would also enhance prospects for regional integration.

In recognition of the need for infrastructure improvements, a number of new international interconnection projects are under consideration that would contribute to regional power market integration.

- Currently, the GCC countries are unable to trade with other MENA countries because they are not physically interconnected. A key transmission project for the MENA region would be the construction of the proposed Egypt-Saudi Arabia high-voltage direct current (HVDC) interconnection. Such a project would open the door to trade between GCC countries and ECI countries, and ultimately beyond to the Maghreb and Europe.

- A new HVDC undersea interconnection is being considered between the United Arab Emirates and the Islamic Republic of Iran.

Box 4.1

Priority Policy and Institutional Reforms in the MENA Region

Policy reforms

- Support ongoing reforms relating to legislative and regulatory frameworks for the gradual establishment of national electricity markets, evolving toward an integrated regional market in MENA
- Develop tools and conditions for market opening
- Establish regulations that guarantee third-party access to the network
- Establish common rules for the use of networks within the framework of an integrated regional market
- Develop a common methodology for calculating transmission tariffs and border congestion management
- Develop market rules to govern trade in the regional electricity market
- Develop a regional grid code to establish minimum technical standards for national power markets
- Strengthen dialogue on the concept of open market with industry representatives to increase their involvement in the market reform process
- Establish rules and identify the authorities dedicated to the resolution of international disputes
- Identify training needs and implement training activities to accompany the process of market opening
- Develop technical databases and identify the capacity of networks and interconnections
- Assess the potential of all types of renewable energy and study ways to export renewable energy within MENA and beyond to Europe
- Identify and analyze methods to support renewable energy development

Institutional reforms

- Establish a committee of national regulatory authorities to enable the sharing of experiences, harmonization of regulatory procedures, and development of common methodologies; encourage the development of "best practices"
- Define the function, identify the structure, and assist in the formation of the regional TSO/market facilitator(s)
- Define the function, identify the structure, and assist in the formation of the Regional Electricity Market (REM) Regulatory Committee
- Define the function, identify the structure, and assist in the formation of a REM association of TSOs

This interconnection could open the door to electricity trade between the Islamic Republic of Iran and the GCC. The Islamic Republic of Iran provides a gateway to further trade through its international interconnections with Afghanistan, Armenia, Azerbaijan, Iraq, Pakistan, Turkey, and Turkmenistan.

- Consideration has been given to establishing interconnections between Algeria and Spain, Algeria and Italy, and Tunisia and Italy (Sicily), with the interconnection between Tunisia and Sicily being the most promising. The plan is to export electricity generated from a new power plant through a 400 kV HVDC submarine cable (30 km on land and 195 km undersea at a depth of 600 meters). The line's capacity would be 1,000 MW, and commissioning is planned for 2016.[8]

- Closing the Mediterranean Ring would also be a priority for MENA's longer-term regional integration objectives. As noted above, trade cannot currently be conducted between the Maghreb and Libya and points beyond to other ECI countries because Libya is not synchronized with the Maghreb. A test conducted in 2010 to synchronize Libya with the Maghreb failed for a variety of reasons, including frequency control. The Med-ring program is undertaking studies to determine an optimized solution. Such studies will include consideration of combined high-voltage alternate current (HVAC)–HVDC infrastructure improvements. In this sense, the project is likely to be a hybrid, combining a new international interconnection component and a component on reinforcing existing transmission infrastructure in the national electricity systems.

Several issues remain with regard to transmission systems in MENA countries. The ECI provides a good example. Although Egypt, Libya, Jordan, and Syria are synchronized with each other, they are not synchronized with Lebanon, Iraq, and Turkey, and West Bank and Gaza, thus limiting regional integration within the ECI subregion. Numerous studies have been conducted, or are underway, on how best to strengthen national transmission networks and existing cross-border interconnections (box 4.2).

Regional projects tend to be more complex than single-country projects, and financing them can be challenging. To advance the preparation and implementation of electricity integration in the region, two parallel tracks will need to be pursued. First, there is a need to harmonize: (i) technical codes and standards for the national energy systems;

Box 4.2

Potential Transmission and Interconnection Lines

Reinforce the ECI corridor. This will depend in part on how the Libya–Maghreb synchronization proceeds. Pending the results of these studies, a number of projects may emerge, including:

- Building a second transmission line between Egypt and Jordan
- Upgrading the interconnection between Syria and Lebanon
- Upgrading the interconnection between Iraq and Syria
- Constructing a new interconnection from Jordan to the West Bank
- Constructing a new interconnection from Egypt to Gaza
- Building interconnection with Turkey

Although fully interconnected and synchronized (except in Libya), transfers of large amounts of power across northern Africa are not currently possible. For example, Algeria–Tunisia transfers are limited to 150 MW. A number of *grid-strengthening projects* are under study in the region, including:

- A 400 kV interconnection between Morocco and Algeria
- A 400 kV interconnection between Algeria and Tunisia
- A 400 kV interconnection between Tunisia and Libya

(ii) regulation in the national energy sectors; (iii) goals and milestones for energy sector reform, particularly where it relates to open access and consistent and fair pricing of transport; (iv) energy pricing and taxation; and (v) development of an independent process and procedure for resolving disputes relating to regional energy transactions. Second, it will be important to foster specific cross-border transactions. The private sector can play a pivotal role in cooperating with the public sector to promote and finance regional projects like those listed above. While the public sector can take the lead in developing an enabling environment for energy trade and private sector participation, the private sector can contribute financing, especially to generation projects intended for cross-border trade. Effective cooperation between the public and private sectors will require the formulation of financing and implementation schemes that mitigate the bottlenecks to private sector participation and offer viable options for ownership, financing structures, and risk coverage.

Information and Communications Technology

The information and communications technology (ICT) sector can play an important role in fostering MENA's regional and global integration. Broadband infrastructure and services contribute directly to domestic productivity, competitiveness, job creation, and economic diversification. Low-cost and high-quality ICT services (network and applications) reduce transaction costs and allow flexible firm locations. Voice and data communications enable faster service delivery and reduce unnecessary travel time. ICT contributes to the competitiveness of the services sector, bringing positive spillover effects to less technology-intensive industries.

The telecommunications sector has become one of the region's main sources of FDI (United Nations 2008). Between 2000 and 2009, the sector attracted almost 70 percent of regional investment (around US\$ 42 billion). The main trigger for this interregional flow of capital has been the introduction of competition in mobile telecommunications markets since the end of the 1990s, with most cross-regional investment focused on mobile operators.

Countries that liberalized first or more aggressively—such as Egypt, Iraq, Jordan, Morocco, and Saudi Arabia—have received the largest FDI inflows from within and outside the region (primarily from Europe and South Africa). By contrast, capital inflows have been limited in countries where there has been no or only timid liberalization—including Lebanon, Libya, and Syria. However, even in difficult environments where investment carries political risks, such as Iraq, announcements of additional licenses have attracted interest from multiple potential bidders.

The opening of mobile markets has attracted intraregional and external flows through greenfield investments in new licenses and cross-border mergers and acquisitions of national operators and regional groups. Recent major transactions include the Qtel acquisition of 51 percent of Wataniya for US\$ 3.7 billion, and the merger of Russia's Vipelcom and Egypt's Weather Investments (Orascom), valued at US\$ 6.5 billion. The value of these transactions increased as a result of the scarcity of licenses. Major greenfield transactions include three mobile licenses acquired by Qtel and Zain in Iraq for US\$ 1.25 billion each. Between 2000 and 2009, greenfield investments attracted a total of US\$ 19.5 billion in investment.[9]

The opening of mobile markets[10] has spurred the creation of large regional transnational operators (TNO) in MENA, led by Wataniya (Kuwait), Orascom (Egypt), Etisalat (Unite Arab Emirates), and Zain/ Qtel (Kuwait/Qatar) (table 4.2). This has strengthened regional

Table 4.2   Regional TNO Groups' Subsidiaries and Subscriber Outreach Abroad

Company	Country of origin	Clients in own country (millions)	Number of countries with subsidiaries (>20% ownership)	Subscriber outreach abroad (millions)
Qatar Telecom/ Wataniya	Qatar	2.1	14	67.7
Orascom	Egypt, Arab Rep.	30.5	9	52.7
Zain	Kuwait	2.0	6	37.6
Saudi Telecom	Saudi Arabia	25.0	7	23.8
Maroc Telecom	Morocco	17.0	4	3.2
Batelco	Bahrain	0.8	6	10.0
Etisalat	United Arab Emirates	7.5	17	39.7

Source: Telegeography GlobalComms Database 2011.

integration in the mobile telecommunications sector, in a manner similar to that of the EU, where regional groups have expanded through all of the EU countries. More than 30 percent of users in MENA, over 130 million people, are served by companies controlled by regional TNOs.

Despite the success generated by the liberalization of mobile markets across the region, the fixed and broadband market has remained closed or quasi-closed to competition (table 4.3). With limited exceptions, opening of this market has been restricted largely to the service layer (with no infrastructure). When infrastructure competition has been allowed, restrictions in the number of licenses and regulatory or *de facto* conditions have generally resulted in limited or no competition. This has resulted in low interregional Internet traffic. Much of the Middle East's Internet traffic (88 percent) goes to Europe and, though inter-regional connectivity has increased, by 2011 it accounted for only 3 percent of total Internet capacity deployed in the Middle East (Telegeography 2011). The lack of competition and regionally integrated operators in broadband services has resulted in high prices, limited investment, and low coverage and breadth of services. Just 5 percent of MENA's population has access to fixed broadband infrastructure, one-third of the level in Eastern Europe and less than 10 percent of that achieved in the EU.

Based on the success of the mobile sector, MENA has an opportunity to enhance fixed and broadband sector performance by further integrat-ing the telecommunications sector. Opening the underdeveloped fixed and broadband market to regional competition could reduce costs,

Table 4.3   Competition in MENA's Fixed Infrastructure and Mobile Markets

	Fixed broadband infrastructure	Mobile market	Mobile broadband[a]
Algeria	Monopoly	Competition	No
Bahrain	Competition	Competition	Competition
Egypt, Arab Rep.	Monopoly	Competition	Competition
Iran, Islamic Rep.	Monopoly	Competition	No
Iraq	Duopoly (state owned)	Competition	No
Jordan	Competition	Competition	Monopoly
Kuwait	Monopoly	Competition	Competition
Lebanon	Monopoly	Duopoly (state owned)	No
Libya	Monopoly	Duoploy (state owned)	Duopoly (state owned)
Morocco	Competition	Competition	Competition
Oman	Duopoly	Duopoly	Duopoly
Qatar	Duopoly (limited)	Duopoly	Duopoly
Saudi Arabia	Competition (limited)	Competition	Competition
Syria	Monopoly	Duopoly (state owned)	Duopoly
Tunisia	Duopoly	Competitive	Monopoly
United Arab Emirates	Duopoly (limited)	Duopoly	Duopoly
West Bank and Gaza	Monopoly	Competition	Competition
Yemen, Rep.	Monopoly	Competition	Monopoly

Source: Telegeography GlobalComms Database 2011.
a. Competition implies that there are three or more 3G (mobile broadband) licenses. All of these countries currently have only three licenses.

improve service quality, and inspire the development of new industries such as business process outsourcing (box 4.3). Increased regional integration and capital inflows from the mobile market could be extended to the sector as a whole if the fixed infrastructure and broadband market were opened to new entrants. There is ample evidence that regional TNOs would be willing to expand in both mobile and fixed markets, which are seen as complementary to the mobile market. The large customer base already created in MENA by the mobile industry is likely to spur acceleration in mobile broadband over the next few years, as customers move from simple devices to smartphones. Mobile broadband will only be possible, however, if mobile operators have access to fixed transmission infrastructure. For this to happen, governments will need to: (i) fully open the fixed and broadband market, including international gateways and backbone infrastructure; (ii) work toward further regulatory harmonization; and (iii) converge toward a common ICT policy framework. These measures are discussed in more detail below.

A new wave of liberalization that includes the fixed market is needed. Experience in other parts of the world, such as Eastern Europe, suggests

Box 4.3

The IT-BPO Industry as a New Opportunity in the MENA Region

The global information technology and business process outsourcing (IT-BPO) industry is a growing area in the services trade that holds tremendous potential for job creation in MENA. The global industry is forecast to grow fourfold, reaching US$ 1.5 trillion by 2020. BPO is less knowledge intensive than other IT industries such as software and hardware development. It is relatively easy to start up BPO businesses as long as affordable infrastructure and ICT services, such as broadband Internet, are readily available.

Some countries in the MENA region have begun to take advantage of IT-BPO opportunities. According to A.T. Kearney's Global Services Location Index for 2011, which ranks the top 50 business relocation destinations, Egypt ranked fourth after India, China, and Malaysia. The United Arab Emirates ranked 15th and Morocco 37th. In Egypt, revenues from the BPO industry were estimated at around US$ 1.3 billion in 2010. Cairo is becoming a major BPO hub in the region with its affordable, skilled, and multilingual (in Arabic, French, and English) labor force. The region's multilingual capacities and strategic location number among its strengths in developing the IT-BPO industry. Moreover, its geographical proximity and similar time zone to the EU provide advantages for European companies in outsourcing business process work to the MENA region.

Source: Kearney 2011.

that full market opening can lead to explosive growth in fixed and mobile backbone investment and subscriber penetration. Countries in the EU have implemented a policy of "full liberalization," involving the removal of all entry barriers in the telecommunications sector as a whole. By contrast, no countries in MENA have implemented full liberalization in telecommunications. Jordan and Bahrain have adopted a market structure similar to that in the EU and Turkey (which opened its sector in 2008), but all other MENA countries have entry barriers in some form.

A common policy and regulatory framework will help regional integration by allowing economies of scale (for example, in terminals and spectrum network equipment), similar use of standards, and cross-regional products and services. Harmonization would also be likely to spur cross-regional FDI, particularly in the broadband segment as it becomes more regionally integrated. Common investment standards would help reduce discretion on the part of national governments and create a stable investment framework. Regulatory harmonization would reduce regulatory uncertainty, lowering the cost of capital required by investors. To be effective, regulatory harmonization would need to address the following areas: (i) licensing; (ii) interconnection; (iii) access to essential facilities (such as cable landing stations and international gateways); (iv) entry of utilities into the telecommunications sector; and (v) regional arbitration (such as a supranational common arbitration system for adjudication of telecommunications sector investment disputes).

MENA has the technical capability to adopt these reforms and deepen regional ICT integration. The region has already established excellent institutions that promote international cooperation at a technical level. These institutions include a network of telecommunications regulators, the Arab Regulators Network (ARAGNET), and an ICT development and cooperation agency, the Arab Information and Communications Technology Organization (AICTO). The International Telecommunication Union's regional body in Cairo plays a major role in promoting regional integration in the sector. Telecommunications regulators in MENA's francophone countries are cooperating under the auspices of an organization that brings together francophone regulators (*Réseau Francophone de la Régulation des Télecommunications*, FRATEL). A range of regional and multilateral financiers are supporting ICT development. In addition, countries in the MENA region can work with various institutions under the framework of national and regional cooperation programs to achieve deeper integration of their markets and domestic policies in the telecommunications sector, unleashing the potential of broadband for the next decade of development in the Arab world.

Notes

1. More than 70 percent of the world's dry cargo maritime trade is now carried in boxes.

2. The high-speed line under construction between Riyadh and Jedda, via Mecca, is for passengers only.

3. Under the landlord port model, a port authority owned by the state (national, regional, or municipal) provides the infrastructure of the port and bears the

costs of its development (dredging approach channels, constructing breakwaters, berths, flat storage areas, and access roads or rail links), while private firms handle cargoes and bear the cost of cranes and other handling equipment, storage sheds, and silos. The port authority awards the operating concession, normally through a competitive process for a period of years long enough to amortize the investment in operating equipment. The port may award a single operating concession or several, competing with one another or specializing in different categories of freight (such as containers, liquid bulks, and dry bulks). The landlord model has been adopted over the past two decades in ports, not only in MENA but around the world, replacing in most cases full state ownership and operation combined under a single public entity. The results have been highly favorable almost everywhere, thanks to the separation of commercial functions (such as cargo handling services) open to competition *in* the market or at least *for* the market, from the ownership of infrastructure that often has a strong element of natural monopoly. Egypt has not yet completed this institutional and functional separation, to the detriment of its ports' performance.

4. The goal of the ongoing Mediterranean Ring project is to interconnect the electric transmission systems of the countries that encircle the Mediterranean Sea to increase energy security in the region and enable more efficient and lower-cost power production. The project envisions linking power systems from Spain to Morocco through the remaining Maghreb countries, on to Egypt and the Mashreq countries, and on to Turkey. From Turkey, the ring would link back into the European grid via Greece or through newly interconnected Eastern European country grids.

5. The fuel cost of US$ 48/MWh is based on a gas price of US$ 6.82/GJ, consistent with a crude oil price scenario of US$ 75/bbl.

6. Estimates provided by the firm Frost and Sullivan.

7. The market participant would have to show it has the necessary expertise and financial resources to conduct the roles and responsibilities in a manner consistent with those specified in the governance documents.

8. See the minutes of the Eighteenth Annual Meeting of Medelec in Algiers, September 27–29, 2010.

9. Public-Private Infrastructure Advisory Facility 2010.

10. The timeline for mobile markets opening to competition was as follows: 1998–99 (Egypt, Kuwait, Morocco, and West Bank and Gaza); 2000–01 (Algeria, Jordan, and the Republic of Yemen); 2002–03 (Iraq and Tunisia); 2004–05 (the Islamic Republic of Iran, Oman, and Saudi Arabia); and 2006–08 (Qatar and the United Arab Emirates).

References

A.T. Kearney. 2011. *Offshoring Opportunities amid Economic Turbulence. The A.T. Kearney Global Services Location Index 2011.* Information Technology Industry Development Agency (ITIDA), Giza, Egypt. http://www.itida.gov .eg/En/Pages/home.aspx.

Logistics Performance Index. 2012. World Bank, Washington, DC.

Telegeography GlobalComms Database. 2011. http://telegeography.com/research-services/index.html.

United Nations. 2008. *Foreign Direct Investment Report.* Economic and Social Commission for Western Asia (ESCWA). http://www.escwa.un.org/ information/publications/edit/upload/edgd-09-TP2.pdf.

CHAPTER 5

Trade Facilitation and Logistics

The ease with which goods can be moved internationally is critical to national competitiveness. As part of this agenda, trade facilitation and logistics reforms aim to address the links between investments in hard infrastructure and the policy actions needed to facilitate trade flows and improve the efficiency of supply chains linking domestic producers and buyers to international partners, whether in the same region or in distant markets.

The concept of logistics performance helps shed light on the various dimensions of supply efficiency and how they are influenced by national endowments and policies. There are three main pillars of logistics performance: (i) the availability and quality of trade-related infrastructure such as ports, airports, roads, and railroads; (ii) the favorability and transparency of trade procedures implemented by customs and other border control agencies; and (iii) the development and quality of logistics services such as trucking, warehousing, freight forwarding, shipping and customs agent services, and value-added logistics services.

A country's logistics performance and its ability to connect to international markets thus depend on a number of nationally and regionally focused policy and institutional measures. Priority areas include: (i) regional integration and development of trade corridors, including border-crossing and transit regimes; (ii) customs reform and trade facilitation; (iii) border management extending beyond customs; (iv) port reform; (v) regulation and development of logistics services such as trucking, third-party logistics, freight forwarding, and warehousing; (vi) development of performance metrics; and (vii) formation of public-private coalitions for reform.

High Trade Costs and Low Logistics Performance

Trade costs are calculated as the price (or tariff) equivalent of the reduction of international trade as compared with the potential implied by domestic production and consumption in the origin and destination markets. Higher bilateral trade costs result in smaller bilateral trade flows. Bilateral trade costs capture a variety of factors: (i) the impact of distance between trade partners; (ii) logistics performance (including costs, delays, and reliability) and facilitation bottlenecks at origin and destination; (iii) the international connectivity of trading countries (for example, the existence of regular maritime or terrestrial services), notably in view of the hub-and-spoke organization of international transportation services such as shipping and air transport; (iv) trade facilitation at the border (including customs and other procedures) for contiguous countries; (v) tariffs; and (vi) nontariff barriers and restrictions to trade (such as quotas and standards).

Trade costs are high in the Middle East and North Africa (MENA) region compared to Western Europe, especially for regional trade. The cost of trade between neighbors is typically twice as high for MENA countries as in Western Europe (table 5.1). Indeed, Maghreb countries face lower trade costs when trading with Europe than when trading among themselves. MENA's trade costs are consistently higher for agricultural products (figure 5.1), reflecting higher transportation costs

Table 5.1   Bilateral Trade Costs for Industrial Products
percent

	Maghreb	Mashreq	GCC	Egypt, Arab Rep.	France/Italy/Spain	Greece
Maghreb	95	152	167	126	75	151
Egypt, Arab Rep.	126	112	111	—	119	163
Mashreq	152	77	96	112	149	185
France/Italy/Spain	75	149	132	119	50	96
Greece	151	185	169	163	96	—
GCC	167	96	69	111	132	169

Source: Shepherd 2011.
Note: — = not available.

Figure 5.1   Trade Costs for Manufactured and Agricultural Goods, Maghreb and Selected European Countries

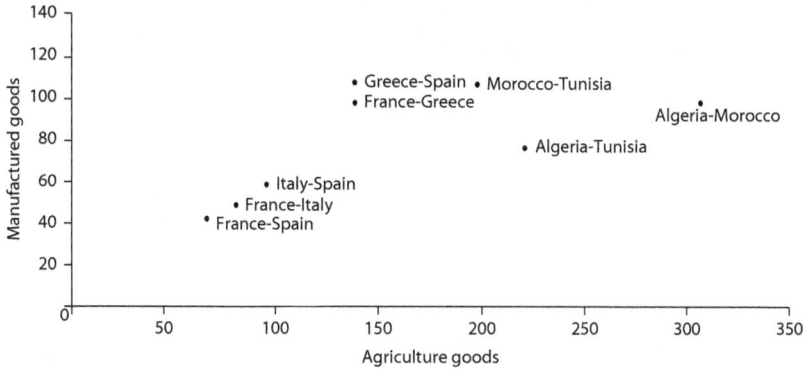

Source: Shepherd 2011.

(per unit value), time sensitivity for perishable products, and potentially the impact of greater border controls and nontariff measures.

To what extent do weaknesses in logistics contribute to these high trade costs? Two indicators specifically measure different aspects of logistics and trade facilitation. The Logistics Performance Index (LPI), developed by the World Bank on the basis of a survey of logistics professionals, scores countries on six key dimensions of logistics performance, including the quality of trade- and transport-related infrastructure, the competence and quality of logistics services, and the efficiency of border clearance procedures. The Liner Shipping Connectivity Index (LSCI), compiled by the United Nations Conference on Trade and Development (UNCTAD), assesses how well a country is served by container shipping services, assigning a high score to countries that host shipping hubs. According to these indicators, MENA fares better on connectivity than on facilitation and logistics (table 5.2). This finding demonstrates that the region's considerable geographical advantages are being hampered by low logistics performance and facilitation bottlenecks.

Though MENA countries have typically underperformed on logistics performance in comparison to countries at a similar level of development in other regions, the region saw significant progress between 2007 and 2008. Morocco, for example, has improved markedly since the first survey in 2007, reflecting meaningful reforms and infrastructure improvements on the ground. Countries that underwent major political transition in 2011, including Tunisia and the Arab Republic of Egypt, generally maintained or improved their scores, which suggests that improvements

Table 5.2   Logistics Performance and Shipping Connectivity

	LSCI 2010 (0–100)	LSCI Rank 2010 (out of 183)	LPI 210 (1–5)	LPI Rank 2010 (out of 165)	LPI 2012 (1–5)	LPI Rank 2012 (out of 155)
France	75	11	3.8	17	3.9	12
Spain	74	12	3.6	25	3.7	20
Italy	60	16	3.6	22	3.7	24
Greece	34	30	3.0	54	2.8	69
Turkey	36	29	3.2	39	3.5	27
Cyprus	16	64	3.1	46	3.2	35
Morocco	49	18	n.a.	n.a.	3.0	50
Algeria	31	35	2.4	130	2.4	125
Tunisia	6	105	2.8	61	3.2	41
Egypt, Arab Rep.	48	20	2.6	92	3.0	57
Lebanon	30	39	3.3	33	2.6	96
United Arab Emirates	63	15	3.6	24	3.8	17
Saudi Arabia	50	17	3.2	40	3.2	37

Sources: Liner Shipping Connectivity Index 2010; Logistics Performance Index 2010, 2012.

in transparency may trump the negative impact of less organized logistics services and supply chains. Trends are less encouraging in the eastern Mediterranean, where logistics performance is considerably weaker to begin with.

Main Logistics Issues across the MENA Region

MENA countries share some common features and constraints that explain some of the region's weaknesses in logistics and trade facilitation. It is therefore important to recognize that these countries have faced different logistics and trade facilitation reform dynamics. The region's countries can be grouped into four main groups in this regard. The first are middle-income countries with some degree of convergence in reforms and facilitation systems, essentially including the parties to the Agadir Agreement for the Establishment of a Free Trade Zone (Egypt, Jordan, Morocco, and Tunisia,) and Algeria. These countries' trade and transportation patterns share a common Mediterranean orientation. The second group consists of the Gulf Cooperation Council (GCC) countries, which are similar to each other and increasingly integrated. The third group includes conflict or post-conflict countries—namely Libya, Iraq, and the Syrian Arab Republic—which have been isolated for decades from the global movement toward trade facilitation and logistics reforms. These countries will need to rebuild their "soft infrastructure" almost from zero. The fourth group includes two least developed countries, the Republic of Yemen and Djibouti, with comparatively rudimentary development of services and border management.

Common Issues
Soft constraints provide the primary explanation for comparatively poor logistics and trade facilitation performance in MENA, whether measured with synthetic indices like the LPI or by actual cross-border time data provided by port and customs authorities. For example, container dwell time in Morocco or Tunisia is about 1 week, much higher than benchmarks for countries of the Organisation for Economic Co-operation and Development (3 days) or emerging economies in Asia (4 days for Malaysia and 2.5 days for transit time in Shanghai).

Markets for logistics services, including trucking, are fragmented by country, with many small providers. There are few incentives to maintain good quality, and regulatory bottlenecks prevent the emergence of modern logistics companies. Government ownership of logistics companies is extensive, which has slowed down the transformation of the services sector.

Difficult political relationships among some countries in the region further restrict the physical movement of goods and people. Relatively few active trade corridors exist between MENA countries, less so in the wake of recent events associated with the Arab Spring movement. Before the Arab Spring, the most active corridors included Tunisia-Libya, Turkey-Syria-Jordan, Jordan-Iraq, and within the GCC. While there are not many limitations on the movement of people and vehicles under normal circumstances, control of corridors does delay trade. Apart from the Tunisia-Libya experiment at Raz Jair, there is no cross-border coordination between countries. Often there are wide "no man's land" areas between posts. There are many controls on either side of each border, including for security purposes. A World Bank mission in 2009 counted about ten controls, distributed equally on each side, to cross from Damascus, Syria, to Amman, Jordan.

Apart from the GCC, which is a single market, and in an embryonic way the Arab Maghreb Union (AMU), there is little communication between technical agencies such as customs and transportation on developing a common trade and transport facilitation framework. For example, there is no agreement on a transit regime to facilitate movement from origin to destination along several borders, although several countries are parties to the International Road Transport (TIR) Convention, which aims to help achieve such agreements.[1] Several groups are encouraging common trade and transport frameworks, however. The Transport Group of the Western Mediterranean (GTMO) 5+5, supported by a think tank in Barcelona (CETMO), has played an important role in mapping needs and supporting dialogue across countries in the western Mediterranean and beyond, with a primary focus on transport networks. The World Customs Organization (WCO) is the current platform for exchange among customs experts in the region; its MENA chapter is headed by Morocco.

Agadir Agreement Countries and Algeria

Trade infrastructure. As discussed in chapter 4, Morocco has had the most consistent program for developing trade-related infrastructure for all modes of transportation. Port capacity has doubled over the past decade, thanks to successful investment in Tanger-Med (mostly, but not only, for transshipment) and to capacity investment and reorganization in Casablanca. Port management was modernized through the separation of landlord and operational activities and through private sector participation, first in Tangier and now in Casablanca. Railroad and toll road networks have been expanded and modernized and will soon be continuous from Agadir to the Algerian border.

Algeria has recently undertaken major investments in trade-related infrastructure, and its motorway system now runs from east to west. Ambitious programs are being implemented in the railway sector. Several projects are being considered to address port capacity constraints, notably in Algiers. Unbundling of operational responsibilities and private participation is less comprehensive than in neighboring countries, however.

Tunisia has implemented a number of reforms, including unbundling port operations. However, port capacity is limited (mostly in Radès-Tunis), and the government has yet to decide whether to expand an existing port or build a new one. The motorway system is incomplete toward the borders, and railroad networks need upgrading.

Egypt has become a major transshipment hub and hosts several efficient, state-of-the-art port facilities. The country has also invested in the modernization of air transport infrastructure. Given high density and congestion in major economic centers, there are serious concerns with inland trade logistics, related to services like trucking as well as the availability of infrastructure for multimodal logistics or transfer operations.

Jordan has invested in road infrastructure on its major corridors linking the Amman region to neighboring countries and the Red Sea (Aqaba).

These investments have included infrastructure to reduce congestion in the city and to improve traffic flow in Aqaba. Jordan is also undertaking a major railroad network development project.

Customs. Significant customs reforms in the Maghreb have been driven largely by the countries' European Union (EU) Association Agreements and the need to converge with the EU's customs code and processes. Morocco and Algeria have developed their own customs software, while Tunisia combined its own software with implementation of Automated System for Customs Data (ASYCUDA) World software.[2] Customs reform in Egypt and Jordan has been supported by U.S.-funded technical assistance and is considered to be broadly successful. Jordan is often held up as a showcase for implementation of ASYCUDA World. Despite common WCO-sanctioned principles, there are obvious differences between countries in eastern MENA and in the Maghreb with regard to customs management philosophy (with a higher emphasis on security in Jordan) and control or implementation techniques. This may not be a practical problem for most trade operations, but it may become a problem if some degree of harmonization is sought among MENA countries. Jordan has adopted idiosyncratic special regimes (including a "golden list" of traders with simplified procedures and a global positioning system [GPS]-based transit system) that differ significantly from the European techniques that have been adopted by Maghreb countries.

In recent years, the focus of customs reforms has shifted toward risk management and special regimes for authorized operators. Tunisia began early, and "offshore" companies have been operating there with customs privileges since the 1970s. Since 2005, Morocco has introduced schemes to allow warehousing, inventory management, and production under customs, with great success. The new customs code, introduced in 2011, has introduced authorized operators and rationalized the risk management channels for standard operations. Egypt, Jordan, and Tunisia have implemented similar programs, but less systematically. One of the main challenges is to introduce transparency in the provision of such privileges to avoid the risk that authorized operators would abuse these facilitation schemes.

So far, relatively little has been done to foster customs cooperation among MENA countries. Customs officials have periodic meetings and have agreed to pool resources to provide training for countries such as Libya and Mauritania. Morocco and Tunisia have agreed on mutual access to clearance data, so that real-time information from the exporting country can help speed up clearances in the importing country. Should this initiative be scaled up to a larger group of countries, it could be particularly beneficial to regional trade.

Services. Many countries in the region are struggling to varying degrees with the modernization of logistics services. These services include agents such as brokers or shipping agents, truckers, warehousing, and, increasingly, value-added services that integrate individual operations for the shippers or even "3PLs" (third-party logistics providers) performing operations that were previously conducted in-house (such as inventory management and packaging).

Trucking reform is a major area of concern in Egypt, Morocco, and Tunisia. These countries dropped government intervention in loading with little impact on services; "informality" and low compliance, combined with relatively small distances, has prevented the emergence of a network of high-quality medium-sized transport operators. Intermediary professions (such as brokers and agents) also tend to be fragmented and provide services with little attention to quality. Nationality requirements for brokers (except in Morocco) have led the industry to be dominated by a small number of domestic operators.

There are two success stories, however. In 2007, Jordan implemented an innovative loading-by-appointment system at the port of Aqaba, which forced truckers to operate in formal companies. This radically changed the market structure and loading factors of trucking operations on the corridor serving Amman and Iraq. Similarly, Morocco has reformed its logistics policy regime, encouraging international and domestic investment in logistics and triggering the development of new services catering to the manufacturing industry, in parallel with the "old" fragmented trucking and brokerage sector. The policy facilitates the development of logistics zones (in Casablanca, Tangier, and elsewhere), removes obstacles to foreign direct investment (FDI) in the logistics sector, and establishes new customs regimes suitable for logistics activities.

Gulf Cooperation Council

As discussed elsewhere in this report, the Gulf countries stand apart from the developing MENA countries with regard to performance in trade facilitation, infrastructure development, and logistics. The United Arab Emirates is known to have developed a world-class logistics hub in Dubai. Furthermore, the GCC is the most advanced model of subregional integration in the broader MENA region.

Libya, Syria, and Iraq

Historically, Libya and Syria were not part of regional agreements or participants in forums (such as the WCO or, for Libya, the WTO) that would have helped them gain access to international experience or implement good trade facilitation practices. Border procedures in these countries have been only partially automated and could be described as nontransparent. In Syria, trade procedures were district-specific. Excessive intermediation in services has been encouraged to stimulate employment. For example, Syria has maintained a form of queuing system for truckers and brokerage monopolies for retired customs officials. Such practices were phased out years ago in the Agadir countries.

Libya and Syria have both undergone significant reform during the last decade. Syria has facilitated private sector participation in key areas (such as the port concession in Latakia) and has initiated customs reforms with the implementation of ASYCUDA World and reconstruction of border facilities to ease regional trade. The EU and France have provided some technical assistance to Syria's customs service as part of the preparation of an Association Agreement.[3] Libya has recently engaged in an ambitious infrastructure program and in some reform of logistics-related activities. Tunisia has offered good cooperation and transfer of knowledge on border management, resulting in a fairly effective cross-border arrangement to facilitate the fast-growing movement of goods and vehicles at the Raz Jair border crossing. Libya has adopted liberal policies on air transportation to and from other Arab countries.

Capacity Building Projects

Most trade facilitation and logistics reforms and projects undertaken thus far in MENA have been initiated and implemented with a focus on trade with Europe and Asia. However, more attention is now being given to facilitating cross-border trade within the region, especially within the GCC, Maghreb, and Mashreq subregions. Specific cross-border project needs include the design of transit or cross-border procedures and facilities and exchange of information.

International organizations have helped a number of countries in the region to build capacity for trade facilitation and logistics. These organizations include the World Bank, European Investment Bank (EIB), Asian Development Bank, EU, and United States Agency for International Development (USAID). In addition to country-specific projects, there are three relevant subregional projects: the Mashreq Corridor Program, the Maghreb Corridor Program, and Logismed (promoted by the EIB). The World Bank has been heavily involved in helping several MENA countries build the software and institutions necessary for providing modern services, including through:

- Countrywide strategies on facilitation and logistics: Morocco (2006), Tunisia (2008–10), and Egypt (initial assessment in 2011);
- Targeted technical assistance such as port facilitation in Casablanca, Morocco, and the definition of trucking reform options in Egypt;
- An export promotion program in Tunisia (disbursed in three tranches since 2000), including an important component on trade facilitation, which focuses on the use of information technology (TunisTradenet) and support for customs reform;
- Development policy lending on competitiveness, including trade facilitation components: Tunisia (2009), Morocco (2010);
- Initiation of technical assistance on the reduction of nontariff measures (Morocco, Egypt); and
- Trade and Transport Facilitation Assessments: Djibouti (2011–12), with a focus on developing the corridor to Ethiopia; Republic of Yemen (2010, postponed).

Mashreq Corridor Program

A 2010 World Bank study on regional cross-border trade facilitation and infrastructure in the Mashreq (which includes Iraq, Jordan, Lebanon, Syria, and West Bank and Gaza) identified several issues with regard to regional trade facilitation, logistics, and transport, including: (i) lack of coordination in the implementation of national projects and policies; (ii) limited integration of cross-border facilities or procedures between countries; (iii) low quality of trucking fleets, limited use of TIR, and long delays at borders with third countries; (iv) missing or inadequate transport infrastructure and properly equipped border-crossing facilities; and (v) lack of subregional economic or corridor management arrangements.

The study made recommendations for addressing these issues and constraints based on logistics audits and regional trade corridors. Proposed reforms included coordinated and phased policy and regulatory changes, as well as transport and border-crossing infrastructure investments that would benefit trade in identified transport corridors: (i) the North-South corridor linking Europe to Saudi Arabia and the Gulf states via Jordan, Syria, and Turkey; and (ii) the East-West corridors linking Mediterranean Mashreq ports to Iraq and Jordan to Iraq. It is estimated that implementation of this program, which aims to remove cross-border constraints, would increase trade by about US$ 15 billion per year by 2020. It is also expected to generate 250,000 permanent jobs, mostly in occupations with a higher-than-average share of female workers, as well as 14,000 temporary jobs in the construction industry (World Bank 2012).

The study's action plan of short-, medium-, and long-term reform actions was translated into a 15-year regional Cross-Border Trade Facilitation and Infrastructure Plan (CBTFI, 2013–27) for Mashreq countries. This plan is to be implemented with support from the World Bank and other development partners (including the EIB, EU, Agence Française de Développement, Islamic Development Bank or IsDB, Arab Fund, Kuwait Fund, Saudi Fund, Japan International Cooperation Agency, and USAID). The plan is estimated to cost about US$ 16 billion in total, with an initial five-year project (2013–17) of about US$ 2.5 billion.

Maghreb Corridor Program

In 2010, the World Bank initiated a regional study on trade and transport facilitation and infrastructure for AMU countries. This initiative is sponsored by the Secretariat of the AMU and involves partner organizations such as the African Development Bank (AfDB) and the EIB. The focus of the work includes: (i) regional trade infrastructure and missing links; (ii) facilitation of regional trade, including through information and single window services; (iii) trade corridors, including land borders and transit regimes; (iv) development and integration of logistics services; (v) critical capacity reenforcement at the national level; (vi) investment in shipping, ports, and railroads; (vii) linkages with other trade policy issues such as nontariff measures; and (viii) capacity needs for regional institutions.

Draft action plans were discussed with policy makers and stakeholders in Algiers in April 2011 and further elaborated with a group of experts in Tunis later the same year. The final action plan was approved by the concerned Ministers of the Maghreb countries and AMU at a ministerial workshop held in Rabat in June 2012, and preparation of a Maghreb trade facilitation and infrastructure program to be supported by international and bilateral partners (including the World Bank, AfDB, EIB, IsDB, and Arab Funds) has been initiated.

The Logismed Initiative

The EIB and the Marseilles Center for Regional Integration are promoting the concept of a network of Euro-Mediterranean logistics platforms in connection with the European "Motorways of the Sea" project. This project would create logistics platforms that would provide a raft of services bearing a quality label covering the whole logistics value chain, from training to the provision of administrative and management services. The project is expected to develop a training network in the logistics field, aimed at creating a regional pool of specialists and experts. In its first phase, the project aims to: (i) develop a network for logistics training in the Mediterranean basin with similar curricula; and (ii) create networks of teachers and professionals with an interest in further training in transport and logistics.

Conclusions

Trade facilitation and logistics is an important part of the effort to improve global and regional integration in MENA. Unfortunately, MENA countries typically lag behind countries at similar income levels in Asia and Latin America on logistics efficiency. As a result, many MENA countries are not taking full advantage of the relatively good shipping connectivity in the Mediterranean or of their proximity to European markets.

Implementation of remedial policies and investments must first be considered at the national level. Needs are higher in countries that have been affected by internal conflicts, such as Iraq, Libya, and Syria. Middle-income countries with comparatively diversified production and export bases, such as Jordan, Morocco, and Tunisia, have progressed further in implementing trade facilitation and logistics services reforms, and their experiences may benefit other countries in the region.

In the Mediterranean, convergence toward European regulations and border management processes, notably as part of the EU Association Agreement process, is likely to remain a major driver of reform. Several important subregional dynamics are expected to support and complement national efforts to harmonize with EU standards. In the western part of the region, the Maghreb countries can integrate further and facilitate regional trade under the AMU for border management and services. In the east, regional trade could be facilitated through a corridor-based initiative involving the Mashreq countries.

National capacity building and reform initiatives can also benefit from subregional activities. From a practical standpoint, the participation of experts from other Arab countries in capacity building initiatives would be highly desirable, particularly in Iraq, Libya, and Syria. Libya's reconstruction could benefit directly from a focus on regional Maghreb integration.

For example, customs activities could be relaunched on the basis of a convergence of codes, tools, and border management principles with other Maghreb countries.

Notes

1. Jordan, Morocco, Syria, and Tunisia are members, but it is used exclusively for trade with third countries (such as European countries or Turkey).
2. The Automated System for Customs Data is a computerized system designed by UNCTAD to administer a country's customs.
3. This association agreement did not materialize following the change in direction of reforms in Syria.

References

Liner Shipping Connectivity Index. 2010. United Nations Conference on Trade and Development, Geneva, Switzerland.

Logistics Performance Index. 2010. World Bank, Washington, DC.

Logistics Performance Index. 2012. World Bank, Washington, DC.

Shepherd, Benjamin A. 2011. "Trade Costs in the Maghreb: World Bank MNA Region."

World Bank. 2012. "Mashreq Trade and Integration Program (P120105): Project Concept Note." Draft report (February). World Bank, Washington, DC.

CHAPTER 6

Preferential Trade Agreements

Over the past 15 years, there has been an unprecedented increase in the number, breadth, and depth of Preferential Trade Agreements (PTAs) in the world. The number of PTAs has doubled during this period, reaching 278 at the end of 2010. PTAs have been employed in all regions, including Middle East and North Africa (MENA). Bilateral PTAs are becoming the norm, often between countries in different regions. South-South PTAs represent about two-thirds of all PTAs and North-South PTAs about one-quarter (Chauffour and Kleimann, forthcoming).

PTAs are pursued for diverse motives, beyond that of simply gaining market access. Modern PTAs tend to address regulatory and policy issues that go well beyond the removal of tariff and quantitative restrictions to trade in goods and services.[1] Deep PTAs extend to rules and disciplines on various regulatory border and behind-the-border policies, such as competition policy, investment policy, government procurement, and intellectual property. Often, PTAs include provisions relating to trade in services and encompass commitments that either exceed those accepted at the multilateral level or that are outside the current World Trade Organization (WTO) mandate. PTAs have the potential to highlight contentious issues, such as the role of the state, subsidies, and soft budget constraints, which provide special advantages to national firms, particularly in the services sector. A major advantage of PTAs is that they tend to spur beyond-the-border regulatory reform, which itself contributes to improving competitiveness and productivity in the participating nations.

PTAs present significant opportunities and challenges for reform-minded governments. The main challenge is the potential complexity of overlapping regulatory regimes arising from an array of PTAs, which can render trade relations less transparent and more unpredictable (Chauffour and Maur 2011). Each PTA tends to create its own web of regulatory rules that coexist alongside multilateral rules. On the other hand, PTAs offer the potential to boost trade and investment flows by expanding market access and can serve as powerful instruments to lock in wide-ranging policy and regulatory reforms.

Theoretical analyses have raised a number of concerns about the proliferation of PTAs in recent years: trade diversion could occur, broader external trade liberalization could stall, and multilateralism could be undermined. Freund and Ornelas (2010) found that the first two concerns were not supported by empirical analysis, and the third area has yet to be properly tested. A recent review of a number of PTAs (Chauffour and Maur 2011) shows that PTA partners trade more internally than would be expected in the absence of a PTA, and that the impact on extra-PTA trade is largely positive. Almost all PTA members seem to trade more with each other than would otherwise be expected from a typical trading relationship between countries with similar incomes. However, one cannot infer from this that it was the PTA alone that led to these outcomes.

Several countries in MENA have entered into a variety of multilateral, regional, and bilateral trade PTAs in an attempt to foster deeper global and regional economic integration. This chapter examines the implementation of the main trade agreements in MENA, and, to the extent feasible, assesses their impact on trade and other aspects of economic performance. This chapter discusses the results of new analysis undertaken to assess the impacts of major trade agreements (notably PAFTA and accords with the European Union or EU and United States) based on country case studies, a before-and-after analysis, and a gravity model.

PTA Implementation—A Lot More Can Be Done

There are several motivations for signing a PTA agreement, beyond just market access. The multiplicity of objectives makes the implementation of PTAs more challenging. Experience to date shows that the status of implementation of PTAs varies widely across countries in the MENA region as well as in the world.

Motivations and Implementation Status

MENA countries have become members of several different PTAs. These agreements exist within the region (Gulf Cooperation Council or GCC, Pan Arab Free Trade Agreement or PAFTA, Arab Maghreb Union or AMU), with the EU (Euro-Mediterranean Free Trade Area Agreement), and with the United States (Free Trade Agreement or FTA). This creates a web of overlapping arrangements (figure A.1), often reflecting different tariff schedules, sectoral and/or product coverage, implementation timeframes, rules of origin, customs procedures, and other requirements.

At the outset, PTAs in the MENA region were designed primarily to foster broader market access. As they have evolved, PTAs increasingly aim to achieve broader economic objectives such as locking in domestic policy reforms, promoting international standards, and delivering regional public goods. Appendix A provides a brief description of the main regional and bilateral trade agreements in the MENA region.

Experience to date suggests that implementation of PTAs has been variable. The GCC has been fairly well implemented, but for others progress is mixed. On balance, more progress has been made in implementing PTAs between MENA countries and other regions of the world than in implementing those among countries of the region. For many MENA countries, the multitude of PTAs and their increasing scope and complexity have proven cumbersome to manage and implement.

Pan-Arab free trade area. According to Hoekman and Zarrouk (2009), PAFTA has been beneficial due to the removal of tariffs on intra-PAFTA trade and to a marked improvement in customs clearance procedures. These are the main findings of a survey conducted by the authors, which focused on trading firms in nine PAFTA countries. The survey covered official trade and tax policies, administrative requirements confronted by traders, and the costs and quality of transport infrastructure.

Arab Maghreb Union. None of the key measures in the AMU agreement have been fully implemented, and intra-Maghreb trade has remained low. The subregion still lags behind other subregions with respect to the ease of doing business and logistics performance, with significant variation among countries. Overall, the subregion includes two countries that are quite advanced in trade openness (Morocco and Tunisia) and two major countries that are not yet WTO members (Algeria and Libya). This heterogeneity in country characteristics might also explain the degree of concentration and the pattern of trade and investment diversification within the region.

Gulf Cooperation Council. The GCC's progress on PTA implementation can be divided into two phases. From 1981 to 2001, the emphasis was on coordination of trade policies. Since 2002, the emphasis has been on full economic integration. Throughout this time, institutional mechanisms have remained fairly stable, albeit with a growing amount of technical work underlying the activities of the major bodies.

The coordination phase of the GCC was devoted mainly to the achievement of a free trade area among member states, agreement on common policies in selected areas, and establishment of specialized agencies. By 1983, participating countries had implemented the exemption of most GCC products from customs duties and simplified customs procedures for GCC products and for travelers between GCC countries. By 1990, retail and wholesale trade were opened for participation by any GCC national. The 1981 agreement had also set out the objectives of free movement of labor and capital and full national treatment regarding ownership and economic activity in any GCC country. However, the extent of technical work required to operationalize these commitments was significant and, with some exceptions (as in domestic trade), progress in these areas was slow.

The GCC declared common market status in 2008. The new common market arrangement was implemented gradually. GCC nationals can now move freely among member countries using a personal identification card. Moreover, GCC members recently approved a waiver of the visa requirement for expatriates with valid professional visas in other Gulf countries. With regard to direct investment, member states have progressively expanded the list of sectors open for cross-border investment. Current areas include retail and wholesale trade, recruitment offices, car rentals, and most cultural activities.[2] The number of business licenses granted to GCC nationals (outside each member country) reached 13,356 in 2005, almost double the number in 1998. Also, restrictions on stock ownership and property possession by GCC citizens have been significantly reduced during the last two years, leading to a surge in intraregional capital flows. Over time, the specification of sectors that are open for inward investment has shifted from a positive list of permitted sectors to a negative list of sectors that are not permitted. The negative list currently includes four activities: religious services, foreign manpower supply, certain commercial agencies, and certain social services, such as elderly and handicapped care. Nevertheless, the specific regulatory measures needed for active cross-border participation in all other sectors are still being established on a case-by-case basis.

The establishment of a single currency in the GCC, initiated under the 2001 GCC Economic Summit, was envisioned for 2010 but has been postponed pending further studies and harmonization measures. This deferral followed from the decision of two members (Oman and the United Arab Emirates) to opt out, and, more recently, from concerns about other members' readiness following the financial crisis in Europe and mounting pressures on the euro. Nevertheless, a GCC Monetary Council including the four remaining member countries has been established in Riyadh to continue working on the technical steps for monetary union.

Euro-Mediterranean free trade area agreement. The 1995 Barcelona Conference set the ambitious goal of establishing Euromed, which would include EU and MENA countries. This goal was to be achieved through Association Agreements between the EU and MENA countries and free trade agreements among MENA countries. So far, trade agreements have been signed between the EU and six MENA countries.

For example, the EU has cooperated with Jordan and Morocco to promote cross-regional investment since the signature of the respective Association Agreements. As a result of reforms linked to the Association Agreements, investment restrictions in Jordan have been substantially reduced. Several initiatives have been undertaken in Morocco to support private sector development, including a program of direct support called the Euro-Morocco Business Enterprise program, the Quality Support Project, the Program to Provide Guarantees (PAIGAM), and the Program of Support for Professional Associations (PAAP).

Implementation of the Euromed FTA has not been as aggressive in all countries. In the Arab Republic of Egypt, for example, little action has been taken to open up investment as envisioned in the Association Agreement. There are two main reasons for this slow progress. First, investment liberalization is generally challenging to tackle in a concerted manner. Second, it has been difficult to reach an agreement on the right of establishment concept, which is still subject to discussion between the EU and Egypt in the context of services negotiations.

Issues Related to PTA Implementation

In 2011, the World Bank carried out an assessment of PTA policy implementation based on 13 country case studies (Chaffour and Kleimann, forthcoming), including three from the MENA region (Egypt, Jordan, and Morocco). Seven PTA policy areas were covered under this study: sanitary and phytosanitary measures (SPS), trade facilitation measures, government procurement, competition policy, services liberalization, intellectual property rights (IPR), and rules of origin. All but the last of these are behind-the-border polices. The study examines how and to what extent entering into a PTA has effectively driven or supported domestic policy as well as institutional and regulatory reforms.

One of the key findings of the study is the need to understand PTAs as "living instruments" that are subject to continuous adjustments, and to provide for institutional feedback mechanisms. The study also finds that implementing cross-border trade facilitation measures is time consuming and costly, and requires substantial institutional capacity. It is not surprising, therefore, to see that progress has been uneven and depends on the scope and depth of the PTA provisions as well as the participating countries' institutional capacity and political economy considerations. Box 6.1 summarizes the achievements and challenges in all seven areas mentioned above.

PTA Impact—Mixed Effects

Are there real benefits that arise from PTAs? To answer this question, it is necessary to understand the impacts of such agreements. Yet clearly identifying the impacts of PTAs is challenging given that many factors influence trade and investment flows but cannot be controlled for in practice. Accordingly, it is difficult to disentangle the effects of regional trade agreements from other factors that affect trade. This section should therefore be treated cautiously and viewed as an attempt to provide estimates that are by no means definitive, using a variety of (qualitative and quantitative) techniques, including drawing on the findings of country case studies.

Lower Protection, Stronger Reform, and Higher Investment

Case study results suggest that PTAs have a positive impact on trade, reform, and investment flows. A series of case studies of PTAs in the MENA region, prepared by Chauffour and Maur (2011), finds that the implementation of such agreements has had a strong impact on these countries, both on the rules governing trade and investment and on actual economic performance.

Box 6.1

Implementation of Preferential Trade Agreements for Development

Implementing PTAs poses a number of challenges. A World Bank assessment of PTA policy implementation, which drew from 13 country case studies (Chauffour and Kleimann forthcoming), found the following:

Sanitary and Phytosanitary Measures: SPS provisions in PTAs vary greatly in degree of specificity and detail, level of ambition, applicability of dispute settlement mechanisms, and whether the rules provide for binding legal commitments or have an aspirational character. Developing countries' records in implementing SPS commitments contained in PTAs have been mixed, at best. The SPS requirements of many trading partners of developing countries represent the single most important barrier to their agriculture and food exports. The country case studies demonstrate, however, that bilateral and regional cooperation, as mandated by PTAs, has made a significant contribution to the upgrade of developing countries' SPS systems—at least with regard to certain priority sectors.

Trade Facilitation and Customs Reform: Despite the challenges faced by governments in implementing policies and institutions in these areas, many countries have made considerable progress in upgrading their trade infrastructure to regional and international standards. These achievements have required large public investments and have been facilitated by technical and financial assistance from northern PTA partners, regional and international organizations, and bilateral development partners.

Government Procurement: Provisions on government procurement in PTAs vary greatly in the strength of legal language and detail of commitments. Although many countries already have some form of public procurement system in place, the legislation of most developing countries, including the sample countries, requires significant modification in order to comply with any tangible procurement framework established by PTAs. The case studies show that there are severe capacity concerns with regard to developing countries' ability to create and sustain modern, improved procurement processes. Extralegislative measures that translate legal texts into actual procurement practice remain critical. In this respect, it is crucial to conceive the implementation of regulatory procurement provisions as a long-term process that requires a change of culture, deeply rooted habits, and practice over time.

(continued next page)

Box 6.1 *(continued)*

Competition Policy: PTAs display considerable diversity with regard to the scope and substantive provisions related to competition requirements. Implementation and enforcement of national and regional competition laws in the sample countries have been poor. Countries need to overcome implementation challenges associated with anticompetitive market structures, vested interests, and uncertainty about policy implications. Acquisition and transfer of knowledge about policy design and implementation as well as hard, time-bound obligations can help to overcome these challenges.

Trade and Investment in Services: There has been limited progress in this area, and it has not been covered extensively in the PTA countries. Generally speaking, the successful implementation of sectoral services liberalization is likely to be facilitated by several cross-cutting factors, including ex-ante impact assessments of different sector and mode-of-supply reforms; involvement of sectoral regulators in PTA negotiations; institutionalization of cooperation between domestic regulators at a high level; and provision of targeted technical and financial assistance by partner countries and international organizations to address institutional capacity issues.

Intellectual Property Rights (IPR): All countries in the study sample, including MENA countries, have made significant progress in legislative efforts to comply with obligations under the trade-related aspects of intellectual property rights (TRIPS) Agreement and TRIPS+ in their PTAs. Yet every case study showcases the significant institutional challenges and high budgetary costs associated with enforcing the new IPR legal frameworks. Effective IPR enforcement, in any country, requires a wide range of skills and expertise and strong coordination mechanisms among national institutions dealing with IPR enforcement. This highlights the need for technical and financial assistance from PTA partner countries and international organizations.

Rules of Origin: The restrictiveness and complexity of rules of origin vary greatly among PTAs, with North American Free Trade Agreement (NAFTA) and EU rules among the toughest. The case studies provide anecdotal evidence of the difficulties faced by developing countries' exporters in meeting these requirements. They also show that the deliberate relaxation of origin rules, as through cumulation provisions, can significantly boost developing countries' exports, if such measures are designed with partner countries' production and export capacities in mind. The EU and U.S. PTAs often incorporate "living agreement" instruments, by which "the Parties may direct a working group or subcommittee to review the operation" of the rules of origin "and develop recommendations for amending them in the light of pertinent developments, including changes in technology and production processes, and other relevant factors."

Source: Chauffour and Kleimann, forthcoming.

Level of Protection

As discussed in chapter 2 and consistent with other findings (see, for example, Hoekman and Zarrouk 2009) there is some evidence, looking at the downward trend in the average tariff rate, that PTAs have inspired countries to reform their trade regimes. The MENA country case studies confirm this trend. For example, the maximum applied tariff rate in Egypt declined from more than 100 percent in 1986 to 30 percent in 2009, and the simple weighted average tariff dropped from 19.3 percent in 2005 to 6.3 percent in 2008. These adjustments were accomplished through a series of steps that brought down maximum tariffs and simplified the tariff bands, including through a unilateral tariff reduction process from 2000 on. In 2008, the government of Egypt undertook another round of tariff reductions in response to soaring global food prices.

In Morocco, the simple average tariff was reduced from 34.5 percent in 2000 (when the Association Agreement with the EU entered into force) to 20 percent in 2009. Tariffs were reduced across all sectors of the economy. The common customs duty weighted average was estimated at 17 percent in 2011. Under the tariff preferences provided for in the PTAs, the simple and weighted average tariffs are 9 and 4 percent, respectively, for the EU and 11 and 4 percent, respectively, for the United States.

The GCC succeeded in bringing its common external tariff down to 5 percent on most imported merchandise and zero percent on essential goods (comprising some 400 items). For goods of GCC origin, defined as those with a minimum of 40 percent local value-added and 51 percent local investment, tariffs are waived.[3] Goods that do not meet the rule-of-origin criteria continue to face tariffs similar to those applied to goods from non-GCC markets. Subsequently, the member states have agreed to eliminate the use of tariff escalation for industry protection, switching instead to exemptions for imports of intermediate inputs and equipment for domestic production and export industries (table 6.1).

Reforms and Investment

PTAs have often been used as a tool to promote and lock in economic reforms and increase confidence in the trade liberalization process. To implement the commitments undertaken under their various agreements, Egypt, Jordan, and Morocco needed to pass new legislation, update existing legislation, and take certain regulatory actions. These preferential agreements encouraged reforms covering a wide range of

Table 6.1   GCC Tariff Rates, 2010

percent

	Bahrain	Kuwait	Oman	Qatar	Saudi Arabia	United Arab Emirates
Standard tariff rate	5	5	5	5	5	5
Average MFN rate	5.3	4.9	5.6	5.3	5.0	5.1
Special items						
Tobacco	100	100	100	100	100	100
Alcohol	125	Banned	100	100	Banned	50
Pork	n.a.	Banned	n.a.	Banned	Banned	n.a.
Cars	20	5	10	5	12	5
Exemptions						
Food and medicine	Yes	Yes	Yes	Yes	Yes	Yes
Industry inputs	Yes	Yes	Yes	Yes	Yes	Yes

Source: Rouis and Al-Abdulrazzaq 2010.
Note: n.a. = not applicable.

domains, including environmental protection, the eradication of child labor, improvements in government procurement, and enhancement of IPR. The added value of these agreements in terms of inspiring new legislation is important.

Not all the PTAs in MENA have had the same impact on fostering broad-based reform. In Egypt, for example, the EU Association Agreement played the most meaningful role in encouraging reforms, including those going beyond border measures. PTAs have shifted the Egyptian government's focus from demand-related problems in foreign markets (such as nontariff barriers and high tariff revenue) to domestic issues such as trade facilitation. In so doing, the PTAs have provided indirect pressure for further trade and enterprise reforms. In addition, the EU Association Agreement has created significant momentum for reform in specific areas, including SPS measures, which has had a positive spillover on Egyptian exports in general.

Total FDI has risen sharply in MENA over the past decade, particularly since 2003 (World Bank 2011, figure 3.4). The bulk of FDI comes from within the MENA region, essentially from the GCC. The contributions of the EU and United States have been relatively small. PTAs have had a more modest impact on FDI flows. None of the PTAs—with the exception of the EU Association Agreement and European Free Trade Association (EFTA) and, to a lesser extent, the Turkey FTA—have included specific provisions on FDI and capital transfers. In Egypt, there was a surge in FDI, but this was related more to low labor costs, a huge domestic market, and general improvements in the business environ-ment. It is worth noting that Egypt's rise in FDI, which began in 2004, did not coincide with the conclusion or implementation of any PTA, but rather with the launch of wide-ranging economic reforms in 2004 and with the establishment of the Ministry of Investment in the same year.

The qualifying industrial zones in Jordan and Egypt were more directly associated with increases in FDI. In Egypt, duty-free access to the United States has led investors from India and Turkey—two countries that have no duty-free access to the United States and are major exporters of ready-made garments—to establish their own plants and factories in Egypt.

In Jordan, the Qualifying Industrial Zone (QIZ) has been the only foreign trade agreement to encourage substantial FDI. This was the case especially in the early 2000s, when dozens of new garment factories were set up in the kingdom under the scheme. FDI into QIZs increased from US$ 13 million in 1999 to its highest level of US$ 345 million in 2007, the majority of which came from Asian investors relocating to Jordan to avoid U.S. quotas. In fact, the vast majority of FDI projects during this time were in real estate and tourism development, while investment related to the EU-Jordan Association Agreement or to the Jordan-US FTA (apart from the QIZ) was extremely limited.

The findings of the country case studies are similar to those arising from the before-and-after analysis carried out for the purpose of this study. Egypt and Morocco seem to have benefited from the PTA with the EU, and Jordan and Morocco from the PTA with the United States (IPR: figure 6.1; tables C.27 and C.28). It is difficult to draw strong conclusions regarding causality, as many factors are at play, notably the implementation of economic reforms and investment promotion measures that were unrelated to the PTAs in these countries.

How PTAs are designed makes a difference in terms of their contribu-tion to trade and beyond-the-border reforms. Differences in the rules of origin across different PTAs can inadvertently inhibit trade within the region. For example, the rules of origin applied by the EU and the United States to FTAs signed with Arab countries pose a problem for the even-tual integration of the Arab region. Exporters in countries that have signed FTAs with the EU and the United States (Morocco, for instance) would have to meet different rules when selling in the EU and the United States. They would be able to cumulate import inputs only from members of the Agadir agreement (Jordan, Egypt, Morocco, and Tunisia), but they would not be able to count these inputs toward fulfilling their

Figure 6.1   Change in FDI for Countries with PTAs (US$ millions)

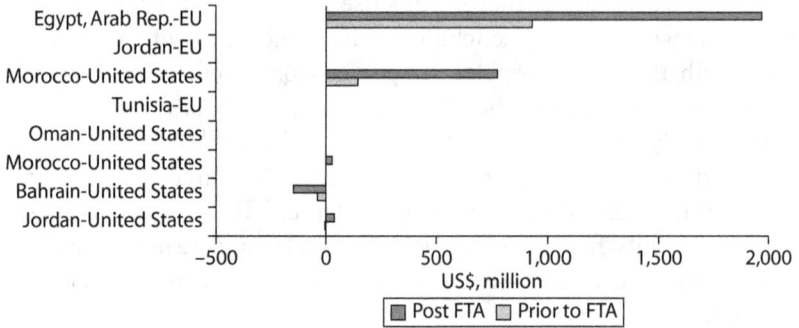

Source: See figures C.3 and C.4.
Note: Figure represents the change from 3-year average before entry into force to 3-year average after entry into force.

U.S. rules of origin requirements. Similarly, European value-added would count toward European exports, but not for those to the United States, and U.S. value added would not count toward meeting EU requirements. Therefore, the rules of origin systems would not only make trading across borders far more complicated and administratively costly, but would mitigate against efficient operations by Arab producers. A common system for cumulation of origin would foster integration, both regionally and globally, together with more efficient resource use. This purpose would be served by a standard rule that goods containing components from any of the PAFTA members should qualify for preferential treatment among members that have FTAs either with the EU or the United States.

Higher Volume of Trade, but Imports Outpace Exports

Review of the Literature
A number of studies have examined the extent to which intraregional trade flows in MENA are lower than would be expected, given GDP, population, and geography. The findings of these studies are largely ambiguous (Hoekman and Sekkat 2010). Simple shares and trade intensity indexes suggest that intraregional trade is not particularly low and has been expanding, while gravity model analysis tends to conclude that trade is below expectations.

One reason that the impacts of PTAs may be less than hoped for is competition from third parties. A World Bank report (Pigato 2009) noted that preferential agreements with the EU have not, in general, helped

MENA countries withstand competition from China and India. They have provided some assistance in maintaining a market in Europe, but the EU rules of origin may impede MENA's further export growth. They are strict, requiring that goods be processed through at least two stages (known as double transformation) for products to qualify for EU trade preferences. As a result, most of the inputs that MENA producers use for exports to the EU come from Europe. Preferential agreements have thus locked MENA producers into production structures that shelter them from competition and limit their ability to source inputs from more competitive locations.

The Before-and-After Analysis

Isolating and attributing trade flow patterns to particular trade agreements is fraught with conceptual and analytical challenges, but comparing trade flows before and after regional trade agreements enter into force can shed some light on their contribution to trade expansion. It is important to remember, however, that it is not a problem, per se, if imports grow faster or are greater than exports after signing a PTA; what matters is the participating country's overall balance of payments. With this caveat in mind, a before-and-after analysis of trade flows was conducted for the three major agreements affecting the MENA region: Euromed Association Agreements, FTAs with the United States, and PAFTA.

Euromed association agreements. A number of MENA countries have entered into Euromed Association Agreements with the EU to provide reciprocal market access. The first such agreement was concluded with Tunisia, entering into force in March 1998. Subsequently, agreements were signed with Morocco (March 2000), Jordan (May 2002), Egypt (June 2004), Algeria (September 2005), and Lebanon (April 2006). In all six cases, there has been a substantial increase in nonfuel trade volumes after the agreements came into force (figure C.3). It is noteworthy that trade volumes increased at a modest rate for the first three to five years after the agreements came into force, suggesting that several years were required for enterprises to identify new market opportunities and respond to changes in competitive market conditions. Following this initial adjustment period, the rise in total trade was substantial, with trade values doubling in participating countries during 2003–08 (figure 6.2). Only in Morocco did the change in exports exceed the change in imports.

With the exception of Jordan, where exports to the EU have been flat, other MENA countries have registered substantial increases in both

Figure 6.2   Change in PTA Volume of Trade and Share

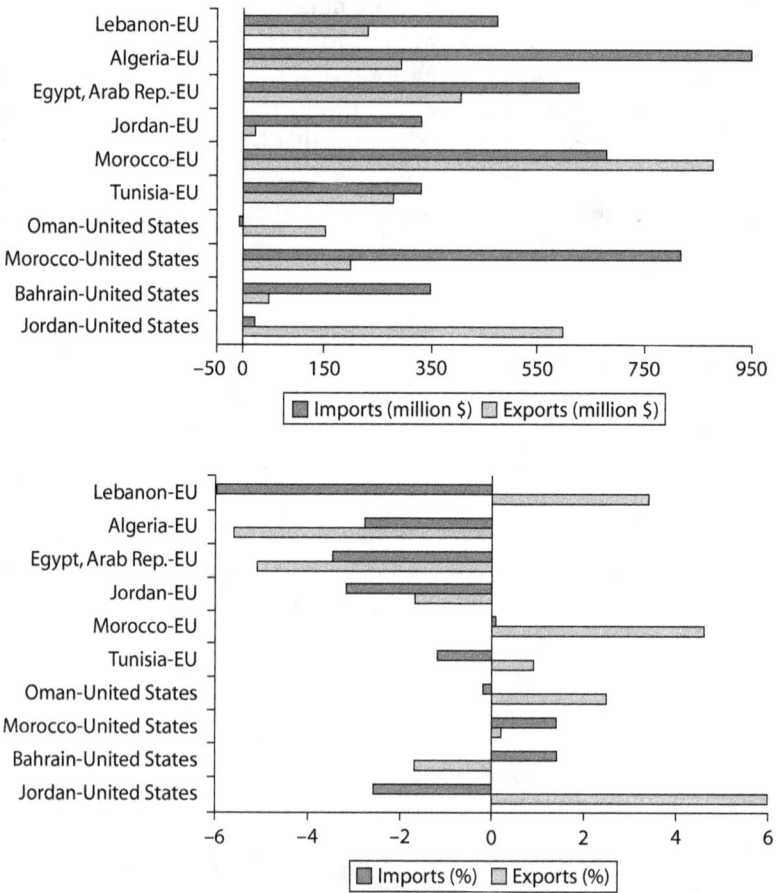

Imports (million $)   Exports (million $)

Imports (%)   Exports (%)

Source: Tables C.27 and C.28.
Note: Figure represents the change from 3-year average before entry into force to 3-year average after entry into force.

imports from and exports to the EU. In all cases (including Algeria for nonfuel trade), the level of imports has surpassed exports by a large margin. This is a worrisome development, as it implies that PTAs have contributed to widening trade imbalances and put pressure on the balance of payments.

Free trade agreements with the United States. MENA countries have entered into a number of PTAs with the United States since 2001, including, among others, agreements with Jordan (December 2001), Morocco

(January 2006), Bahrain (August 2006), and Oman (January 2009). In each of these cases, there has been a substantial increase in total trade with the United States after the FTA has taken effect (figures C.2 and C.4). Oman's experience is an exception, with a substantial reduction in trade— both with the United States and overall—in 2009 and 2010 as a result of the adverse effects of the global financial crisis on commodity demand.

As in the MENA-Euromed case, the growth of imports into the region has vastly outpaced export growth. With the exception of Jordan, exports from the United States to partner MENA countries have outpaced imports by the United States from the MENA countries. In Bahrain, Morocco, and Oman, exports from the United States to the MENA markets more than doubled in value shortly after the relevant FTAs became effective. Moreover, the rate at which imports to the MENA countries from the United States are growing is considerably higher than the rate at which exports to U.S. markets are growing, suggesting that the merchandise trade gap is likely to widen over time. In recent years, total exports to the United States have decelerated largely as a result of competition from Egypt arising from the introduction of QIZs.

Pan-Arab free trade agreement. To what extent is regional trade integra- tion among Arab countries a substitute for wider (that is, MENA-EU and MENA-U.S.) trade integration? The before-and-after analysis of the impact of the PAFTA Trade Agreement (also known as GAFTA, the Greater Arab Free Trade Agreement) suggests that the scope for boosting intraregional trade through PTAs has been rather modest (figure 6.3).

PAFTA involved a progressive lowering of tariffs from 1998 to 2006. Comparing trade flows in 1995 with those in 2000, 2005, and 2007 shows a steady increase in trade within the PAFTA region as interregional tariffs declined. Total trade flows with PAFTA partners increased the most for Saudi Arabia, both for oil and nonfuel trade. A strong response was also registered by the Syrian Arab Republic and the United Arab Emirates. It is interesting to note that the trade response for large MENA economies such as Egypt, Morocco, and Tunisia was relatively modest after PAFTA came into force.

The findings of the before-and-after analysis are consistent with those of two other studies. First, using an augmented gravity model for all MENA countries for which Association Agreements have been signed, Cieślik and Hagemejer (2009) found that although these agreements have significantly increased MENA countries' imports from the EU, they have had a limited impact on their exports to the EU. Second, using

Figure 6.3   Nonfuel Trade with PAFTA Partners (US$ billions)

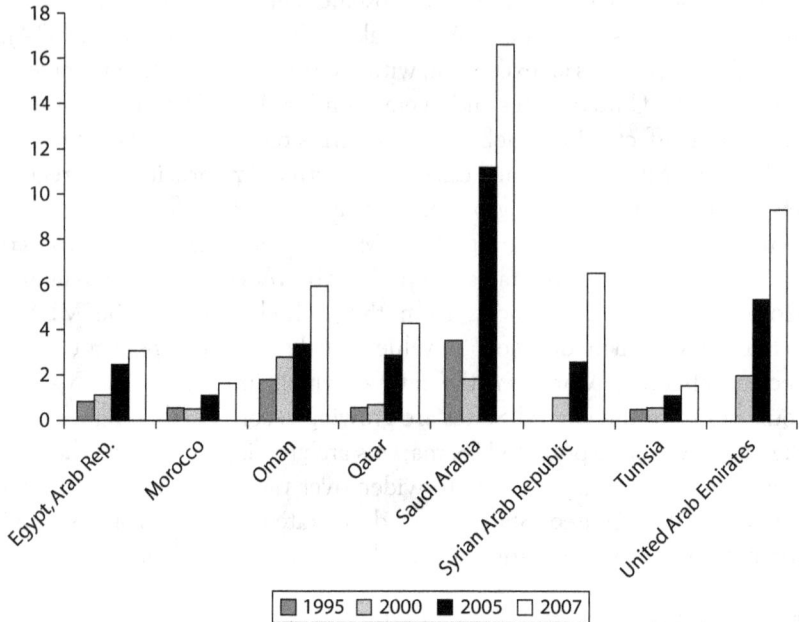

Legend: 1995   2000   2005   2007

Source: WITS 2012.

country case studies, Chauffour and Kleimann (forthcoming) found that PTAs in Morocco have spurred much more rapid growth in imports than in merchandise exports. As a result, the country's trade deficit with the EU increased by more than five times between 1999—the year before the agreement entered into force—and 2009. Similarly, Morocco's trade deficit with the United States increased by more than four times between 2005—the year before the agreement entered into force—and 2009. In the case of Egypt, the absolute value of trade with countries with which it has signed PTAs has increased substantially, though at different rates. At the same time, trade with the rest of the world, and most notably with Asian countries, has increased at a faster rate than trade with countries with which Egypt signed a PTA. The faster growth in imports as compared to exports can be explained in part by the similar production structures across MENA countries. In addition, MENA countries were less prepared to compete in newly opened northern economies. Competition from third markets, notably India and China, also explains why import growth in the MENA region has tended to outpace export growth during the years in which PTAs have come into force.

Gravity Analysis

Using a gravity panel framework, Freund and Portugal-Perez (2012) have estimated the impact of MENA PTAs on trade flows to and from MENA countries. The data panel covers 1994–2009 and corrects for factors such as bilateral distance, common languages, common land borders, and colonial past. The specification also includes dummy variables for two types of PTAs: (i) PTAs whose membership does not include MENA countries (such as the EU); and (ii) those whose membership does include MENA countries. Appendix B provides a detailed discussion of the model, the data, and the results.

The findings from the gravity panel model (table 6.2) suggest that the standard effect of trade agreements on the worldwide exports of their members is an increase of about 21 percent. In the case of MENA, an *additional* increase of about 39 percent is estimated in exports between the United States and MENA countries. However, this effect is driven largely by U.S. preferences granted to Jordan under the QIZ. By contrast, trade preferences granted to MENA countries by the EU seem to lower the standard estimate by about 9 percent. The impact of EU–MENA PTAs compares unfavorably with EU membership, which is estimated to result in an additional increase of about 43 percent. The additional effect on exports of PTAs between MENA countries and Turkey is not statistically significant. On the other hand, intra-MENA PTAs such as the

Table 6.2   Estimated Effects of PTAs on Member Country Exports
percent

PTA (dummy variables)	Regression 1 baseline	Regression 2 MENA exporters	Regression 3 excluding Jordan
PTA (standard effect)	20.8[b]	20.8[b]	21.2[b]
Additional effects			
EU	43.3[b]	43.3[b]	43.0[b]
United States-MENA	39.2[a]	−26.8[b]	
EU-MENA	−8.6[a]	−11.6[b]	−8.8
TURKEY-MENA	2.4	17.1	2.1
PAFTA	24.5[b]	24.5[b]	24.2[b]
AGADIR	28.3[a]	28.3[a]	28.3[a]
United States-MENA (exporters)		237.7[b]	
EU-MENA (exporters)		6.8	
Turkey-MENA (exporters)		−22.1	
United States-MENA (excl. Jordan)			−12.5

Source: Table B.1.

Notes: a. Estimated coefficient significant at 5 percent; b. Estimated coefficient significant at 1 percent.

PAFTA and Agadir have a positive and significant impact on their members' exports, estimated at about 25 and 28 percent more than a standard PTA, respectively.

In sum, the results of the modeling exercise suggest that trade preferences granted to MENA countries by the United States, the EU, and Turkey do not have an additional effect on exports compared to PTAs in general. It is important to note, however, that PAFTA and Agadir do have the effect of expanding the exports of their members, but also that this expansion begins from a low base. Moreover, within PAFTA and Agadir, the findings from the gravity model support the conclusion that countries that are better prepared to compete regionally tend to experience the greatest export gains from participation in regional PTAs.

Conclusion

In MENA, as in the rest of the world, PTAs have been pursued to an increasing degree over the past 15 years to improve trade, investment, and regulatory settings. The design of PTAs has moved beyond the removal of tariff and quantitative restrictions on trade in goods and services to address a wide range of beyond-the-border issues such as SPS measures, trade facilitation measures, government procurement, competition policy, services liberalization, and IPR. The extent to which PTAs have spurred deeper regulatory and institutional reform is one of the most important results of the process, for these have contributed to improvements in the business-enabling environment and have boosted competitiveness along several dimensions.

In principle, PTAs present significant opportunities and challenges for reform-minded governments. Yet implementing PTAs is already a challenge, especially in countries with a fractious political economy environment and weak institutional capacity. Managing the inherent complexity that arises from overlapping and conflicting regulatory regimes is another major challenge. On the other hand, PTAs have been used to expand market access and boost opportunities for trade and investment flows, and PTAs that go beyond border policies are powerful instruments for fostering far-reaching economic policy reform.

Improving PTA enforcement, deepening the agenda, and exploring open regionalism are key steps to maximizing the potential benefits of regional integration. More efforts are needed, particularly within PAFTA and the Arab League, to track progress made in adopting the agreed provisions of regional trade agreements and in helping participating countries make the necessary reforms. Expanding the membership of PTAs could expand the potential benefits of such agreements while boosting incentives to reform, as in the case of the GCC's recent move toward expanded membership. The compatibility of multiple PTAs is also important. Deepening the PTA agenda to address beyond-the-border issues such as subsidies, the role of the government in "strategic" industries, and soft-budget constraints, is critical to fostering fair competition throughout the region. In addition, a standard rule that goods containing components from any of the PAFTA members should qualify for preferential treatment among members that have free trade agreements outside the region would help spur deeper regional integration.

Isolating and attributing the impacts of PTAs is inherently difficult. Tentative findings can be elicited using analytical techniques such as country case studies, before-and-after analysis, and gravity models. First, it appears that PTAs in the MENA region have contributed to or reinforced policy reforms in a number of areas. Second, there is some evidence, particularly in GCC countries and in selected larger MENA economies, that PTAs have helped boost FDI flows. Finally, although PTAs have contributed to an increase in trade volumes, imports have significantly outpaced exports in almost all cases.

Notes

1. See Chauffour and Maur (2011) for deep commitments in selected EU and U.S. PTAs by type of provision. PTAs cover a wide range of policy areas. For instance, Association Agreements with Europe and MENA countries provide a framework for the economic, political, and social dimensions of the EU–MENA countries' partnership. The agreements cover agriculture and sanitary and phytosanitary (SPS) measures, nonagricultural market access (NAMA), technical barriers to trade (TBT), services, customs, investment, competition, IPR, government procurement, environment, and labor markets. The fact that a policy area is covered in an agreement does not imply that commitments have been economically important or that the agreements could be legally enforced.

2. Variations continue to exist among member states, due to the limited transparency of the negative list.

3. Under typical customs unions, the rules of origin are abolished due to the adoption of common external tariffs. In the case of the GCC, this procedure still is followed pending more complete harmonization of external tariffs.

References

Chauffour, Jean-Pierre, and David Kleimann. Forthcoming. *The Implementation of Preferential Trade Agreements for Development: Lessons from 13 World Bank Country Case Studies.* Washington DC: World Bank.

Chauffour, Jean-Pierre, and Jean-Christopher Maur, eds. 2011. *Preferential Trade Agreement Policies for Development: A Handbook.* Washington, DC: World Bank.

Cieślik, Andrzej, and Jan Hagemejer. 2009. "Assessing the Impact of the EU-Sponsored Trade Liberalization in the MENA Countries." *Journal of Economic Integration* 24 (2):344–69.

Freund, Caroline, and Emanuel Ornelas. 2010. "Regional Trade Agreements." *Annual Review of Economics* 2 (1): 139.

Freund, Caroline, and Alberto Portugal-Perez. 2012. "Assessing MENA's Trade Agreements." Middle East and North Africa Working Paper Series No. 55. World Bank, Washington, DC.

Hoekman, Bernard, and Khalid Sekkat. 2010. "Arab Economic Integration: Missing Links." Discussion Paper 7807, Centre for Economic Policy Research, London, U.K.

Hoekman, Bernard, and Jemal Zarrouk. 2009. "Changes in Cross-Border Trade Costs in Pan Arab Free Trade Area." Policy Research Working Paper No. 5031, World Bank, Washington, DC.

Pigato, Miria. 2009. *Strengthening China's and India's Trade and Investment Ties to the Middle East and North Africa.* Orientations in Development Series, World Bank, Washington, D.C.

Rouis, Mustapha, and Ali Al-Abdulrazzaq. 2010. *Economic Integration in the GCC.* Middle East and North Africa Region. Washington, DC: World Bank.

World Bank. 2011. "Towards a New Partnership for Inclusive Growth in the Middle East and North Africa." Arab World Brief No. 5 (May). Washington, DC: World Bank.

WITS (World Integrated Trade Solution). 2012. World Bank, Washington, DC.

CHAPTER 7

Conclusion and Reform Priorities

This chapter summarizes the main findings of the report and provides a broad direction for reform priorities. The major political changes sweeping through the Middle East and North Africa (MENA) region today provide a good opportunity to introduce economic and social reforms that are conducive to economic growth and job creation in an increasingly competitive world. Leaders throughout the region are looking for new measures their governments can take to boost growth and employment. Deeper regional and global economic integration presents valuable opportunities to make the region more attractive to investors, boost productivity and competitiveness, and create opportunities for the good jobs that young people in the region desire and deserve.

Regional Economic Integration—Challenges and Opportunities

The MENA region faces a number of serious economic management challenges and a growing political demand for reform. Economic integration can help address the region's development challenges by strengthening incentives and opportunities for growth, economic diversification, and employment. If managed properly, it can attract the investment needed to generate more and better jobs by improving the enabling environment for both domestic and foreign investment.

Economic theory suggests that how economic integration is pursued matters. If managed in a manner consistent with expanding markets, fostering competitiveness, boosting investment, and facilitating factor flows, it can have considerable positive effects. But if the mechanisms for economic integration lock out more competitive parts of the world or saddle countries with excessively complex border regimes, it can do more harm than good. The theoretical literature is clear, however, that isolation is not a fruitful option (Freund and Ornelas 2010; Winters 2010). Small and isolated economies tend to have less diversified production structures and are more vulnerable to shocks than larger, more economically integrated economies.

Excluding oil and gas, MENA is one of the least globally and regionally integrated regions in the world. The region's share in total world exports of nonoil goods remained under 1 percent during the 1980s and 1990s and under 2 percent over the past decade (figure 7.1). Despite doubling its services exports, MENA's share in total services trade dropped sharply during the 1980s and has since remained stagnant at between 2 and 3 percent. Though on a rising trend, integration within the MENA region is also low, particularly in comparison to other middle- and high-income regions (figure 7.2). Significant progress has been made in reducing tariff

Figure 7.1   MENA's Export Share in the World of Nonfuel Goods and Services

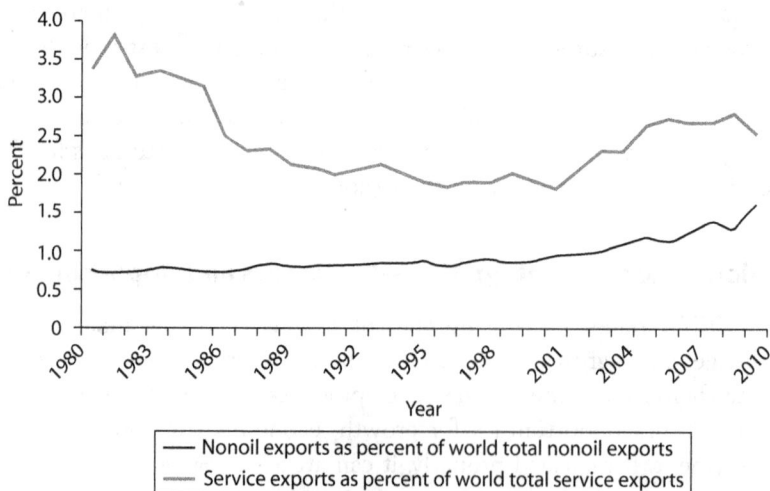

Sources: World Integrated Trade Statistics (WITS) database and World Development Indicators 2012.

Figure 7.2   Share of Exports within Regions

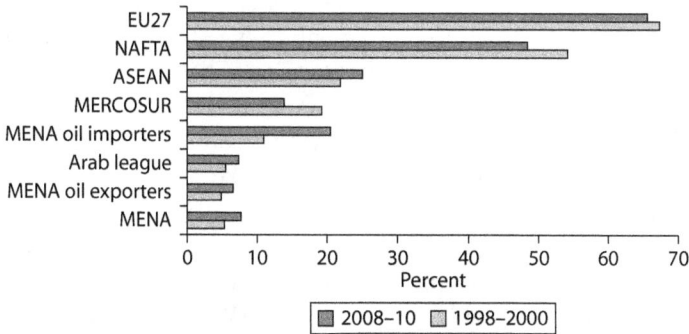

Source: Table C.13.

barriers, but the level of tariff protection vis-à-vis the rest of the world remains high by international standards in MENA, and particularly in North Africa. Nontariff measures have become the most important barriers to trade in goods in the Arab world.

In spite of its comparatively small size, the services sector has been an important source of growth and wealth creation in MENA. Though the services sector is registering strong growth, trade in services is limited and falls outside the scope of Pan Arab Free Trade Agreement (PAFTA) and most other regional Preferential Trade Agreements (PTAs). MENA countries have much to gain from the liberalization of services. As discussed in chapter 3, comprehensive reforms to strengthen competition and streamline regulatory frameworks would yield benefits two to three times greater than those achieved through tariff removal alone (Konan 2003). In particular, opening the services trade in the region would facilitate trade in parts and components and contribute to the emergence of regional production networks.

Backbone services such as telecommunications, financial services, transport, and power are crucial to productivity and international competitiveness. Opening these to competition and trade could help reduce production costs, increase foreign direct investment (FDI), promote knowledge spillovers, and expand markets, all of which would enhance competitiveness. Backbone services also affect a country's and region's ability to competitively export goods and services. For example, efficient port, maritime, and aviation services are crucial to the competitive export of goods (Um, Straub, and Vellutini 2009).

For most MENA countries, the transport sector is key to regional economic integration. Most MENA countries have extensive road networks, but trucking services tend to be unsatisfactory owing to the continued use of outdated vehicles, excess capacity, and weaknesses in the structure of the road freight industry. Several key road and railway links require improvement and/or expansion. The main determinant of trade costs between countries is the port sector, where key determinants of performance include the extent to which countries develop and rely on regional hubs and how well they make use of efficient port concessionaires. Overall, substantial investment and institutional reform will be required to strengthen the capacity and efficiency of MENA's transport infrastructure to support cross-border trade through international and, in particular, regional transport facilities (World Bank 2011).

Economic integration in the power sector is at an early stage of development in MENA. Major initiatives such as the North Africa-Middle East-Europe Mediterranean Power Pool are beginning to take shape, but much remains to be done to introduce competition in the power sector. There are numerous obstacles to electricity trade among Arab countries, including a tight connection between generation demand and supply and the absence of a harmonized regulatory framework with clear rules governing electricity trade. Though Arab countries hold about 30 percent of the world's proven gas reserves, every country (except Qatar) is short of the gas supplies needed to meet current and projected demand. Increased energy integration and trade (for both gas and electricity) would therefore contribute to improvements in the security and sustainability of the region's energy supply. Solar energy holds tremendous potential, but cross-border investment may be needed to realize economies of scale and scope in this area.

While considerable progress has been made in the regional integration of mobile telephony, many important cross-border issues remain to be tackled in the ICT sector, particularly in terms of fixed and mobile broadband infrastructure. Deeper liberalization of fixed and mobile broadband infrastructure, shared information and communications technology (ICT) standards, and regional regulatory harmonization could boost ICT access and performance. To fully reap the benefits of economic cooperation for the region, MENA countries will need to further liberalize the telecommunications market, roll out broadband, develop regionwide ICT regulation, and proactively strengthen competition on backbone networks and international connectivity.

Although implementation of PAFTA has substantially reduced formal trade barriers between MENA countries, facilitation and transport impediments impose greater losses in trade than do formal trade tariffs and quota restrictions. Trade costs can constitute 20 to 40 percent of the final delivered price of nonoil MENA exports. With the declining importance of tariffs in MENA, the quality of trade facilitation has a significant impact on the pattern of trade flows in the world today. Yet many trade opportunities are being lost as a result of inefficient trade facilitation processes and procedures.

Logistics performance varies substantially across countries, with Gulf Cooperation Council (GCC) countries performing reasonably well and nearly all other countries in the region scoring significantly below the average for their income group. Progress in building logistics skills and markets has been constrained by slow and ineffective introduction of risk management, little effort to monitor customs performance at the border, and insufficiently improved facilities at border crossings. Coordination among border agencies within countries is limited, leading to multiple inspections and regulatory requirements at the same border. Transit movements within the Mashreq subregion remain cumbersome due to slow processing of documents and the operation of convoys. Several MENA countries—notably Morocco, Tunisia, the Arab Republic of Egypt, and Jordan—have invested in robust reforms, particularly in customs. Other countries are or should be catching up, and reforms should be expanded to include other border agencies and promote authorized operators to address risk management and integrity issues. Private companies also need to develop modern logistics activities and practices.

A large number of PTAs have been adopted over the past four decades, both within the region and between countries of the region, the European Union (EU), and the United States. The proliferation of PTAs, with their different sector and product coverage, rules of origin, and implementation requirements, poses a formidable implementation challenge for capacity-constrained MENA institutions. This explains in large part why implementation of PTAs has been a gradual process.

Available evidence suggests that implementation of PTAs has had both positive and negative socioeconomic effects in MENA and around the world. PTA implementation has contributed to a significant reduction in trade and investment barriers, spurred behind-the-border economic reforms, and helped boost trade and investment flows. However, the PTAs that MENA states have signed with the EU and the United States have given rise to a far more rapid expansion in imports into the region than exports out of it. Across the region, PTAs have encouraged participating countries to improve their trade infrastructure, harmonize border policies and procedures, and improve supply chains and logistics facilities. If managed judiciously, MENA's PTAs could serve as a stepping-stone to global market integration to the extent that they contribute to more competitive markets, greater economic openness, and a growing reliance on trade in goods and services.

Reform Priorities

While considerable progress has been made, there remains substantial scope for further regional and global economic integration. There are a number of ways to foster economic integration, and in each country considerations of reform readiness, expected benefits, and transition costs will determine the best package and sequence of measures. To strengthen trade in goods, MENA countries could continue to unilaterally reduce most favored nation (MFN) tariffs, with an emphasis on reducing tariff peaks, to the level of the most competitive regions of the world (for example, East Asia). Efforts could also be made to steadily roll back nontariff barriers to trade, which would involve reviewing existing nontariff measures, reducing to the extent possible their scope and remit, and then phasing out those that are not deemed essential for national security purposes.

While there has been strong progress in promoting the free flow of goods, much less has been accomplished in opening up cross-border investment and trade in services. If regional service markets are to emerge, reforms will be required to ease entry and licensing restrictions for both domestic and foreign firms in the services sectors, to promote competition, to harmonize and strengthen regulatory practices and arrangements, and to lower restrictions on the mobility of foreign workers residing in the region. Continued public ownership in some services sectors also represents a potential hurdle to increased regional cooperation, given the caution with which the countries of the region have moved toward privatization. Addressing these issues would have a direct impact on employment, the overriding problem of MENA countries, as services sectors are labor-intensive and thus critical for reducing unemployment.

Within the region, continuous efforts are needed to lower the costs associated with trading across borders. Reducing this burden will require measures to improve the efficiency of border crossing points, including through the harmonization of customs procedures. Outside the GCC, logistics systems will need to be vastly improved. A useful start could be made in this direction by abolishing restrictions on investment in the logistics sector and policies that reserve logistics activities for specific categories of domestic firms. Transport networks will need to be strengthened in order to improve the efficiency of ports and to make better use of regional rail potential. In the power sector, the institutional prerequisites for power trade—unbundling, tariff reform, adequate regulatory oversight, and harmonization of technical standards—need to be put in place alongside strategic investments in regional distribution and transmission networks. Access to ICT is improving rapidly in the region; opening the backbone telecommunications infrastructure to competition and encouraging inward investment in broadband services could bring ICT costs down and make internet services more readily available.

In line with the 2009 Kuwait Arab Economic Summit Declaration, an agreement to open up the services trade among Arab countries could be prepared. Developing such a compact would involve developing a regional strategy for services trade integration, conducting regulatory services audits and evaluating these audits from a regional perspective, and negotiating a pan-Arab agreement in services. Even in advance of comprehensive services trade liberalization, efforts could be made to open up trade in selected services sectors. Key candidate sectors for such early liberalization include: (i) *transportation and logistics*, given the importance of linking land, marine, and air transportation networks to bolster trade, investment, and labor movement within the Arab region; (ii) *banking and finance*, to immediately encourage further intra-Arab investment and facilitate capital movement among Arab countries; and (iii) *communication and information*, in order to enhance the competitive potential of technology enterprises, to develop legislative frameworks related to this sector, and to encourage the private sector to attract investment.

MENA countries have ambitious regional integration objectives. If, as agreed under PAFTA, an Arab Customs Union is to be established by 2015 and an Arab Common Market by 2020, then efforts will need to be made to strengthen the rules and discipline applicable to PAFTA and other regional trade agreements. This would involve strengthening or agreeing on a new set of basic principles for the governance of PAFTA, including strict limits on nontariff measures, meaningful national treatment provisions in the services trade, and an effective framework to guarantee the free movement of labor within the region. This would also involve creating a permanent and independent dispute-settlement mechanism to oversee enforcement, including measures to ensure compliance.

Mechanisms for tracking and enforcing commitments to regional economic integration need to be strengthened. A stronger mandate could be given to the General Secretariat of the League of Arab States to monitor the implementation of members' liberalization commitments, including the dismantling of nontariff measures and the liberalization of services. Regular monitoring of implementation commitments is critical in supporting policy makers' ability to assess and report on the effects of regional integration agreements.

The Arab Spring provides an opportunity for countries to break with the slow reform pace of the past and embark on a faster, deeper, more comprehensive reform agenda, with strong support from the donor community. The partnership launched by the G8 in Deauville, France, in May 2011 to support the historic political and economic change underway in MENA augurs well. This partnership calls on partner countries (Egypt, Jordan, Libya, Morocco, and Tunisia) to formulate homegrown economic and governance reform programs that would enhance domestic competitiveness and promote trade and FDI. In return, the Deauville partners (which include, in addition to the G8 countries, Kuwait, Qatar, Saudi Arabia, Turkey, the United Arab Emirates, and nine international and regional financial institutions) committed themselves to support the partner countries in achieving their goals of economic and political transformation through three strategic pillars: governance, finance, and trade and commerce.

References

Freund, Caroline, and Emanuel Ornelas. 2010. "Regional Trade Agreements." *Annual Review of Economics* 2 (1): 139.

Konan, Denise E. 2003. "Alternative Paths to Prosperity: Trade Liberalization in Egypt and Tunisia." In *Arab Economic Integration: Between Hope and Reality*, ed. Ahmed Galal and Bernard Hoekman, 61–101. Washington, DC: Brookings Institution Press.

Um, Paul Noumba, Stéphane Straub, and Charles Vellutini. 2009. "Infrastructure and Economic Growth in the Middle East and North Africa." Policy Research Working Paper No. 5105, World Bank, Washington, DC.

Winters, L. Alan. 2010. "Regional Integration and Small Countries in South Asia." In *Accelerating Growth and Job Creation in South Asia*, ed. Ejaz Ghani and Sadiq Ahmed, 289–342. New Delhi: Oxford University Press, World Bank.

World Bank. 2011. "Transport." Middle East and North Africa Transport Annual Meetings 2011, Sectoral Note. Washington, DC: World Bank.

Regional and Bilateral Trade Agreements in MENA

Countries in the Middle East and North Africa (MENA) region are involved in a variety of overlapping bilateral and multilateral trade agreements—what is sometimes referred to as a "spaghetti bowl" of trade accords (figure A.1). They are involved in trade agreements with each other (Gulf Cooperation Council or GCC, Pan Arab Free Trade Agreement or PAFTA, and Arab Maghreb Union or AMU), with African states, with the European Union or EU (Euromed), with the United States (Free Trade Agreements or FTA), and with Turkey (table A.1). A total of 11 MENA countries are members of the World Trade Organization or WTO (including the GCC states, Djibouti, the Arab Republic of Egypt, Jordan, Mauritania, Morocco, and Tunisia), and many others are preparing for membership.

For many countries in the region, bilateral and regional trade agreements are understood to be a stepping-stone to broader global trade engagement. Multilateral, regional, and bilateral trade agreements have been pursued in tandem in the region. Several of these intraregional agreements have yet to become fully operational or to fully achieve their stated objectives.

This appendix draws on three subregional studies (on the GCC, Maghreb, and Mashreq) by Mustapha Rouis and others (2010).

Figure A.1 Trade Agreements in the MENA Region

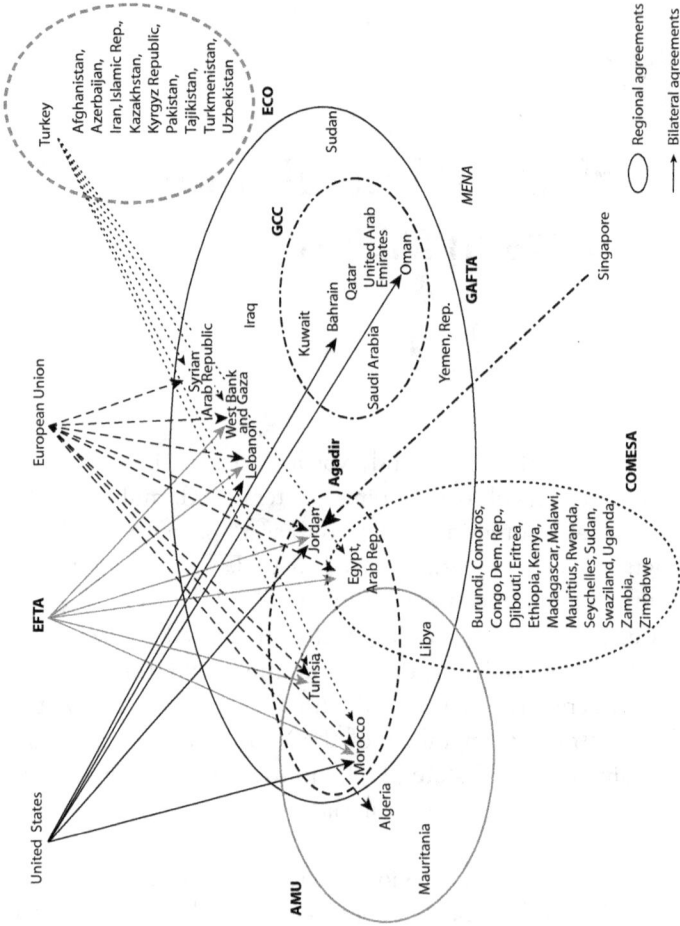

Source: World Bank 2008.

Notes: **AMU**: Arab Maghreb Union (5); **GCC**: Gulf Cooperation Council (6); **GAFTA**: Great Arab Free Trade Agreement (18); **ECO**: Economic Cooperation Organization (10); **COMESA**: Common Market for Eastern and Southern Africa (19); **EFTA**: European Free Trade Association (4), includes Iceland, Switzerland, Norway, and Liechtenstein; **Agadir**: Agadir Agreement for the Establishment of a Free Trade Zone between Arabic Mediterranean Nations (4).

Table A.1   MENA PTA Membership with EU, United States, and Turkey

EU		United States		Turkey	
Country	Entry into force	Country	Entry into force	Country	Entry into force
Algeria	2005	Jordan	2001	Tunisia	2005
Egypt, Arab Rep.	2004	Morocco	2006	Morocco	2006
Jordan	2002	Bahrain	2006	Syrian Arab Republic	2007
Lebanon[a]	2003	Oman	2009	Egypt, Arab Rep.	2007
Morocco	2000			West Bank and Gaza	2005
West Bank and Gaza	1997				
Tunisia	1998				

Sources: European Commission (2007), http://ec.europa.eu/trade/creating-opportunities/bilateral-relations/ regions/euromed/; Office of the United States Trade Representative, http://www.ustr.gov/trade-agreements/ free-trade-agreements; and Customs Tariff information and legislation of Turkey in English, http://www.tariff-tr.com/bul/AraBul2007.aspx?yur=1&a2=Turkey's%20Bilateral%20Agreements.
Note: a. In process of ratification. Interim Agreement for early implementation of trade measures.

League of Arab States

The League of Arab States has historically taken the lead on integration efforts in the region. The League's objective is to "draw closer the relations between member States (22 in total) and co-ordinate collaboration between them, to safeguard their independence and sovereignty, and to consider in a general way the affairs and interests of the Arab countries." Through its various institutions, the Arab League helps to facilitate political, economic, cultural, scientific, and social affairs among its members. Since its inception in 1945, the League has served as a forum for member states to coordinate their policy positions, to deliberate on matters of common concern, and to settle disputes. PAFTA has been a key trade initiative of the League of Arab States.

Pan Arab Free Trade Area

PAFTA, also known as GAFTA, was signed in 1997 and became effective a year later. Its 18 Arab country members account for over 80 percent of total MENA trade, of which less than 10 percent was traded within the region in 2007. The main provisions of PAFTA concern the progressive removal of tariffs (by January 1, 2005) and of nontariff barriers to trade in goods among members (by 2010). More recently, signatories of PAFTA have launched efforts to further integrate trade and investment in services, and to address nontariff measures that restrict trade flows.

The Agadir Agreement

The Agadir Agreement for the Establishment of a Free Trade Zone (Agadir) was signed in Rabat, Morocco, in 2004 and became effective in 2006. Original members include Egypt, Jordan, Morocco, and Tunisia, with the potential to expand to Algeria, Lebanon, Libya, Mauritania, the Syrian Arab Republic, and the West Bank and Gaza. The EU supported the agreement with the aim of establishing a free trade area and as a possible first step in the establishment of Euromed.

The Arab Maghreb Union

The Arab Maghreb Union (AMU) was established in 1989 by five countries (Algeria, Libya, Mauritania, Morocco, and Tunisia). The AMU's aim is to intensify trade among member countries, laying down the foundation for integration and the creation of a North Africa customs union by 1995 and an economic common market by 2000. None of these goals has been achieved.

The Gulf Cooperation Council

The Gulf Cooperation Council, established in May 1981, consists of six Arab countries along the Persian Gulf: Bahrain, Kuwait, Oman, Qatar, Saudi Arabia, and the United Arab Emirates. These countries share many historical and cultural ties and aspire to develop a more diversified economic bloc over time. To accelerate integration efforts, the member states have signed several agreements. An Economic Agreement (December 2001) brought a renewed focus on trade, investment, and various other economic issues. A Customs Union Agreement (2003) aimed to remove restrictions on internal trade and establish common external tariffs. A common market status agreement (2008) aimed to create a single environment where citizens of member countries would enjoy equal rights and privileges, including the rights to move; settle; work; receive social protection, retirement, health, education, and social services; and engage in various economic activities and services. It also calls for unrestricted rights of ownership of property and equity, movement of capital, and similar tax treatment. The establishment of the GCC single currency, planned for 2010, has been postponed.

Euro-Mediterranean Free Trade Area Agreement

The 1995 Barcelona Conference set the ambitious goal of establishing Euromed, which would include EU and MENA countries. This goal is to be achieved through Association Agreements between the EU and MENA countries and FTAs among MENA countries. Thus far, six countries have signed an Association Agreement with the EU: Tunisia in 1995 (which entered into force in March 1998), Morocco in 1996 (which took effect in March 2000), Jordan and West Bank and Gaza in 1997 (which entered into force in May 2002 and 1997, respectively), Egypt in 2001 (which took effect in June 2004), and Algeria and Lebanon in 2002 (which entered into force in September 2005 and April 2006, respectively). Syria initiated discussions in 2008.

Other Agreements

In addition to these regional agreements, several countries have entered into bilateral agreements with each other and with countries outside the region. Jordan has agreements with Bahrain, Egypt, Israel, Morocco, West Bank and Gaza, Sudan, Syria, Tunisia, and the United Arab Emirates, and is negotiating with the GCC. Tunisia has agreements with Egypt, Iraq, Jordan, Libya, and Morocco. Egypt has agreements with Iraq, Jordan, Lebanon, Libya, Morocco, and West Bank and Gaza.

Several countries have entered into bilateral agreements with the European Free Trade Association (EFTA), the EU, the United States, and Turkey. Agreements with the United States include the FTA, Trade and Investment Framework Agreement (TIFA), and Qualifying Industrial Zone (QIZ) agreements with all GCC countries signed between 2003 (Saudi Arabia) and 2006 (Oman). Other countries include Jordan (signed in 2000), Egypt (2004), and Morocco (2004). The GCC as a group is negotiating with a large number of partners across the world, including Australia, EU, India, Japan, Korea, New Zealand, and the United States.

References

Rouis, Mustapha. 2010. *Economic Integration in the Mashreq*. Middle East and North Africa Region. Washington, DC: World Bank.

Rouis, Mustapha, and Ali Al-Abdulrazzaq. 2010. *Economic Integration in the GCC*. Middle East and North Africa Region. Washington, DC: World Bank.

Rouis, Mustapha, and Komlan Kounetsron. 2010. *Economic Integration in the Maghreb*. Middle East and North Africa Region. Washington, DC: World Bank.

World Bank. 2008. *2008 MENA Economic Developments and Prospects: Regional Integration for Global Competitiveness*. Washington, DC: World Bank.

Gravity Model Analysis

The Model

Freund and Portugal-Perez (2012) estimate the following gravity specification:

$$\ln X_{ijt} = \alpha_i + \beta_1 \ln(GDP_{it}) + \beta_2 \ln(GDP_{jt}) + \beta_3 \ln(pcgdp_{it}) + \beta_4 \ln(pcgdp_{jt})$$
$$+ \beta_5 PTA_{ijt} + \beta_6 EU_{ijt} + \beta_7 \ln(PRE\_EU\_PTA_{ijt}) + \beta_7(US\_MENA_{ijt})$$
$$+ \beta_8(EU\_MENA_{ijt}) + \beta_9(TUR\_MENA_{ijt}) + \beta_{10}(IntraMENA_{ijt})$$
$$+ \delta_{ij} + \delta_t + \varepsilon_{ij}$$

where: $\ln X_{ijt}$ are exports of country i to country j in year t; PTA_{ijt} is a dummy variable assuming the value 1 if i and j have a preferential trade agreement in effect in year t and 0 otherwise; EU_{ijt} is a dummy equal to one when countries i and j are members of the European Union (EU) in year t and zero otherwise; $PRE\_EU\_PTA_{ijt}$ is a dummy taking the value 1 if i or j are an EU member and an EU candidate having a PTA in effect in year t and 0 otherwise; GDP and pcgdp stand for gross domestic product and per-capita gross domestic product, respectively; US_MENA, EU_MENA, and TUR_MENA are dummies characterizing PTAs in which either i or j is a MENA country having a PTA with the United States, EU, or Turkey, respectively; IntraMENA$_{ijt}$ is a vector of dummies taking the value of 1 if i and j are two MENA countries having a PTA in effect in year t and 0 otherwise; δ_{ij} are exporter-importer country-pair fixed effects[1] and δ_t are year fixed effects.

The Data

The panel covers the period 1994–2009 and more than 150 countries including almost all (World Bank-defined) MENA countries for which data are available. When constructing MENA aggregates, we exclude Israel from the analysis.

Data for bilateral trade flows are compiled from COMTRADE. Real GDP and real per-capita GDP (at PPP) series are compiled from WDI. Data on preferential trade agreements are collected from CEPII.

The Estimates

Column 1 of table B.1 reports coefficient estimates for the benchmark model. Real GDP are positive and significant. The positive and significant coefficient of PTA can be interpreted as the average effect of trade agreements increasing exports of their members by about 20.8 percent (=exp(0.189)–1). All other PTA coefficients measure the additional effect on their members' exports compared to the average PTA effect. The EU coefficient is also positive and significant and is the highest of all PTA coefficients. It can be translated as EU membership increasing exports by an additional 43.3 percent. PRE_EU_PTA measures the trade effect of preferential agreements between EU members and accessing countries prior joining the EU, which is estimated to increase exports by an additional 12.4 percent compared to a standard PTA.

The positive and significant estimate of US_MENA can be translated as an additional increase in exports by 39.2 percent between the United States and MENA countries having a preferential agreement with the former. Yet, as shown in the last regression, this effect is driven by U.S. preferences granted to Jordan. By opposition, trade preferences granted by the EU have an export-expansion effect that is 8.6 percent lower than the average PTA effect. Although positive, the coefficient of the Turkey-MENA PTA is not significant.

Turning to intra-MENA PTAs, PAFTA and AGADIR are estimated to have a positive and significant impact on their members' exports equal to 24.5 percent and 28.3 percent, respectively. As the panel covers the period 1994–2009, and we are using exporter-importer country-pair fixed

Table B.1 Estimated Effects of PTAs on Exports of Member Countries

	Baseline regression (1)		MENA exports regression (2)		Excluding Jordan regression (3)	
	Coefficient	% change in exports	Coefficient	% change in exports	Coefficient	% change in exports
lnrgdp_rep	1.636 [0.063]***		1.641 [0.064]***		1.637 [0.063]***	
lnrgdp_par	0.237 [0.069]***		0.234 [0.069]***		0.238 [0.069]***	
lnrgdp_pc_rep	−0.016 [0.062]		−0.019 [0.062]		−0.016 [0.062]	
lnrgdp_pc_par	0.992 [0.065]***		0.996 [0.065]***		0.992 [0.065]***	
PTA	0.189 [0.021]***	20.8%	0.189 [0.021]***	20.8%	0.192 [0.021]***	21.2%
EU	0.36 [0.027]***	43.3%	0.36 [0.027]***	43.3%	0.358 [0.027]***	43.0%
PRE_EU_PTA	0.117 [0.027]***	12.4%	0.117 [0.027]***	12.4%	0.115 [0.027]***	12.2%
US_MENA	0.331 [0.163]**	39.2%	−0.312 [0.113]***	−26.8%		
EU_MENA	−0.09 [0.035]**	−8.6%	−0.123 [0.039]***	−11.6%	−0.092 [0.035]***	−8.8%
TURKEY_MENA	0.024 [0.084]	2.4%	0.158 [0.127]	17.1%	0.021 [0.084]	2.1%
PAFTA	0.219 [0.065]***	24.5%	0.219 [0.065]***	24.5%	0.217 [0.065]***	24.2%
AGADIR	0.249 [0.105]**	28.3%	0.249 [0.105]**	28.3%	0.249 [0.105]**	28.3%

(continued next page)

Table B.1 *(continued)*

	Baseline regression (1)		MENA exports regression (2)		Excluding Jordan regression (3)	
	Coefficient	% change in exports	Coefficient	% change in exports	Coefficient	% change in exports
US_MENA_MNAExp			1.217 [0.293]***	237.7%		
EU_MENA_MNAExp			0.066 [0.061]	6.8%		
TUR_MENA_MNAExp			-0.25 [0.160]	-22.1%		
US_MENA_exclJOR					-0.134 [0.094]	-12.5%
Constant	-38.395 [1.714]***		-38.409 [1.714]***		-38.417 [1.714]***	
Observations	220198		220198		220198	
R^2	0.9		0.9		0.9	

Notes: Robust standard errors in brackets; *significant at 10%; **significant at 5%; ***significant at 1%; Dependent variable: log of aggregate exports of country i to j in year t. All regressions have exporter-importer country-pair fixed effects and year fixed effects.

effects, we cannot assess other intra-MENA PTAs that entered into force before 1994, such as the Gulf Cooperation Council (GCC) and the Arab Maghreb Union (AMU), in force since 1981 and 1989, respectively.

To separate out the impact on MENA exports of PTAs with other countries in which they take place, we interact a dummy, MNAExp (taking the value of one when a MENA country is exporter and zero otherwise) with US_MENA, EU_MENA, and TUR_MENA, and incorporate them in the regression. Estimates are reported in column 2 and show that only the United States-MENA agreements have a positive and significant effect on MENA exports.

Finally, the US_MENA dummy is replaced with US_MENA_exclJOR, a dummy that excludes United States' preference to Jordan. Estimates in column 3 show that its coefficient is no longer significant, suggesting that the additional effect of US_MENA trade agreements is driven by preferences to Jordan.

In sum, the results suggest that trade preferences to MENA countries granted by the United States, EU, and Turkey do not have an additional effect compared to other PTAs. In the case of preferences by the EU, they are shown to have a lower impact. By opposition, PAFTA and AGADIR have an additional export-expansion effect on their members.

Note

1. Country-pair fixed effects control for invariant characteristics specific to the country pair such as distance, common language, common border, and common colonizer.

Reference

Freund, Caroline, and Alberto Portugal-Perez. 2012. "Assessing MENA's Trade Agreements." Middle East and North Africa Working Paper Series No. 55. World Bank, Washington, DC.

APPENDIX C

Statistical Tables and Graphs

Data Source and Methodology

The data used for the Middle East and North Africa (MENA) region trade tables are sourced from the World Bank's Integrated Trade Solutions (WITS) database. WITS extracts data from the UN Comtrade database. Export and import data were downloaded for each MENA country. Complete data are not available for all countries. The data are reported by the statistical offices of each country to relevant international organizations. Generally, data that are missing for a country or time period indicate that the reporting country had not reported data for that specific year.

GDP data are sourced from the World Bank's World Development Indicator database in current US$ (series NY.GDP.MKTP.CD).

Tables C.3–C.9 report trade data in 3-year averages for two time periods. The first period covers 1998–2000, and the second period covers 2008–2010. Due to missing data, in some cases the time period was adjusted to provide a 3-year average (see below for more detail). Notable adjustments include:

- Libya data are not available for the two time periods considered.
- Saudi Arabia's second time period data on exports with the MENA Region and subregions are for 2005–07.

- Iraq import data are only available for 2000–2002.
- Djibouti data are only available for 2009.

Tables C.10–C.13 use two the two years for which the most complete data are available, 1995 and 2007, with a few exceptions. For 1995, the Islamic Republic of Iran and Lebanon data are from 1997, and the United Arab Emirates data are from 1993.

Tables C.14–C.17 report trade data by sector (SITC 3) in 3-year averages for two time periods (T1 and T2) without adjustment.

Exports to World

- Bahrain T1 is 2000–02.
- Comoros T2 is 2005–07.
- Djibouti has no data for T1; T2 is 2009.
- Iran T2 is 83.8.
- UAE T1 is 1999–2001.
- Yemen T1 is 2001–03; T2 is 2007–08.

Imports from World

- Bahrain T1 is 2000–02.
- Comoros T2 is 2005–07.
- Djibouti has no data for T1; T2 is only 2009.
- Iran T2 is only 2010.
- Iraq T1 is 2000–02; T2 has no data.
- Kuwait T2 is 2006–08.
- Libya has no data for T1 or T2.
- Mauritania T1 is 2000–02.
- Qatar T2 data is 2007, 2008, and 2010.
- Sudan T2 is 2007–09.
- Syria T1 is 2000–02; T2 is 2006–08.
- UAE T1 is 1999–2001.
- Yemen T1 is 2001–03; T2 is 2007–09.

Exports to MENA

- Bahrain T1 is 2000–02; T2 is 2007–09.
- Iran T2 is 2010.
- Iraq T1 is 2000–02; T2 is 2007–09.
- Kuwait T2 is 2007–09.
- Mauritania T1 is 2000–02.

- Saudi Arabia T1 is 1998; T2 is 2005–07.
- Syria T1 is 2000–02; T2 is 2006–08.
- Yemen T1 is 2001–03; T2 is 2007–09.
- UAE T1 is 1999–2001.

Imports from MENA

- Bahrain T1 is 2000–02; T2 is 2007–09.
- Djibouti T1 has no data; T2 is 2009.
- Iran T2 is 2010.
- Iraq T1 is 2000–02; T2 has no data.
- Kuwait T2 is 2006–09.
- Libya has no data.
- Mauritania T1 is 2000–02.
- Qatar T2 is 2007, 2008, and 2010.
- Syria T1 is 2000–02; T2 is 2006–08.
- Yemen T1 is 2001–03; T2 is 2007–09.
- UAE T1 is 1999–2001.

Exports from Subregion (GCC, Mashreq, Maghreb)

- UAE T1 is 1999–2001.
- Syria T1 is 2000–02; T2 is 2006–08.
- Bahrain T1 is 2000–02.
- Kuwait T1 is 2000–02; T2 is 2007–09.
- Qatar T2 is 2007–09.
- Saudi Arabia T1 is 1998 and 2001; T2 is 2005–07.
- Iraq T1 is 2000–02; T2 is 2007–09.
- Syria T1 is 2000–02; T2 is 2006–08.
- Libya has no data available.
- Yemen T1 is 2001–03.

Imports from Subregion (GCC, Mashreq, Maghreb)

- UAE T1 is 1999–2001.
- Bahrain T1 is 2000–02.
- Kuwait T2 is 2006–08.
- Qatar T2 is 2007, 2008, and 2009.
- Iraq T1 is 2000–02; T2 has no data.
- Syria T1 is 2001–03; T2 is 2006–08.
- Libya has no data available.
- Yemen T1 is 2001–03; T2 is 2007–09.

Table C.1   Country Groupings

Country	MENA	LAS	GCC	Mashreq	Maghreb	Oil exporters	Oil importers	PAFTA	WTO
Algeria	✓	✓			✓	✓		✓	
Bahrain	✓	✓	✓			✓		✓	✓
Comoros		✓							
Djibouti	✓	✓					✓		✓
Egypt, Arab Rep.	✓	✓					✓	✓	✓
Iran, Islamic Rep.	✓					✓			
Iraq	✓	✓		✓		✓		✓	
Jordan	✓	✓		✓			✓	✓	✓
Kuwait	✓	✓	✓			✓		✓	✓
Lebanon	✓	✓		✓			✓	✓	
Libya	✓	✓			✓	✓		✓	
Mauritania		✓			✓				✓
Morocco	✓	✓			✓		✓	✓	✓
Oman	✓	✓	✓			✓		✓	✓
Qatar	✓	✓	✓			✓		✓	✓
Saudi Arabia	✓	✓	✓			✓		✓	✓
Somalia		✓							
Sudan		✓						✓	
Syrian Arab Republic	✓	✓		✓		✓		✓	
Tunisia	✓	✓			✓		✓	✓	✓
United Arab Emirates	✓	✓	✓			✓		✓	✓
West Bank and Gaza	✓	✓		✓			✓	✓	
Yemen, Rep.	✓	✓				✓		✓	
Total	19	22	6	5	5	12	7	18	12

Note: LAS = League of Arab States, GCC = Gulf Cooperation Council.

Table C.2 Social and Economic Indicators

	Population (millions)		Population growth (percent)		GDP (US$ billions)		GDP per capita (US$)	
	2009	2010	2009	2010	2009	2010	2009	2010
Middle East and North Africa	357.23	364.3	2.1	2.0	1,880	2,238	5,669	465
Oil exporters	224.4	229.5	2.4	2.2	1,495	1,816	7,270	8,375
GCC	41.9	43.5	4.6	3.8	878	1,078	23,730	27,452
Bahrain	1.2	1.3	10.6	7.6	21	23	18,589	20,475
Kuwait	2.6	2.7	3.8	3.4	109	133	31,411	37,009
Oman	2.7	2.8	2.8	2.6	47	58	16,255	19,405
Qatar	1.6	1.8	13.5	9.6	98	127	59,545	74,901
Saudi Arabia	26.8	27.4	2.4	2.4	373	435	14,148	16,267
United Arab Emirates	6.9	7.5	11.2	7.9	230	302	53,363	57,884
Developing oil exporters	182.5	186.0	1.9	1.9	617	739	3,494	3,912
Algeria	35.0	35.5	1.5	1.5	141	159	3,926	4,366
Iran, Islamic Rep.	73.1	74.0	1.2	1.1	331	407	4,923	5,449
Iraq	31.1	32.0	3.0	3.0	65	82	2,056	2,531
Syrian Arab Republic	20.0	20.4	2.0	2.0	54	59	2,593	2,823
Yemen, Rep.	23.3	24.1	3.1	3.1	26	31	1,061	1,284
Oil importers	132.8	134.8	1.5	1.5	385	422	2,962	3,215
Oil importers with GCC links	11.0	11.2	1.6	1.6	61	68	5,710	6,255
Djibouti	0.9	0.9	1.9	1.9	1	1	1,305	1,370
Jordan	5.9	6.0	2.2	2.2	25	28	3,987	4,326
Lebanon	4.2	4.2	0.7	0.7	35	39	9,054	10,041

(continued next page)

Table C.2 *(continued)*

	Population (millions)		Population growth (percent)		GDP (US$ billions)		GDP per capita (US$)	
	2009	*2010*	*2009*	*2010*	*2009*	*2010*	*2009*	*2010*
Oil importers with EU links	121.8	123.6	1.5	1.5	324	354	2,714	2,940
Egypt, Arab Rep.	79.7	81.1	1.8	1.7	189	219	2,456	2,808
Morocco	31.6	32.0	1.0	1.0	91	91	2,885	2,861
Tunisia	10.4	10.5	1.1	1.0	44	44	4,171	4,199
Memorandum								
League of Arab States	340	347	2.0	2.2	1,607	1,898	4,731	5,463
East Asia and the Pacific	1,948	1,962	0.7	0.7	6,366	7,631	3,268	3,890
Europe and Central Asia	403	405	0.4	0.4	2,609	3,059	6,467	7,551
Latin America and the Caribbean	576	583	1.1	1.1	4,014	4,982	6,969	8,552
South Asia	1,557	1,579	1.4	1.4	1,701	2,090	1,092	1,323
Sub-Saharan Africa	833	854	2.5	2.5	942	1,098	1,131	1,286

Source: World Bank data.

Table C.3 MENA Total Trade in Goods with World (Annual Average, US$ Billions)

	Exports		Imports		Total[a]	
	1998–2000	2008–10	1998–2000	2008–10	1998–2000	2008–10
MENA region	194.2	824.9	165.4	606.8	359.6	1381.5
Oil exporters	175.3	755.7	120.3	464.9	295.6	1170.4
GCC	114.6	542.5	77.9	342.7	192.5	885.2
Bahrain	5.8	5.8	4.6	13.9	10.4	19.7
Kuwait	13.6	65.8	7.8	21.1	21.4	87.0
Oman	7.9	27.1	5.1	19.6	13.0	46.7
Qatar	6.9	47.9	3.1	24.9	9.9	72.8
Saudi Arabia	55.5	246.5	29.4	105.8	84.9	352.4
United Arab Emirates	25.0	149.3	27.9	157.3	52.9	306.6
Developing oil exporters	60.7	213.2	42.3	122.1	103.1	285.1
Algeria	14.8	60.5	9.2	39.9	24.0	100.4
Iran, Islamic Rep.	20.5	83.8	13.5	54.7	34.0	138.5
Iraq	16.7	50.2	12.3	—	29.0	—
Libya	—	—	—	—	—	—
Syrian Arab Republic	5.4	12.3	4.3	18.1	9.7	30.4
Yemen, Rep.	3.3	6.4	3.0	9.4	6.3	15.9
Oil importers	18.9	69.2	45.1	141.9	64.0	211.1
With GCC links	2.0	9.6	10.3	32.8	12.3	42.4
Djibouti	0.0	0.2	—	0.6	—	0.8
Jordan	1.3	5.7	3.8	15.4	5.1	21.1
Lebanon	0.7	3.7	6.5	16.8	7.2	20.5

(continued next page)

125

Table C.3 (continued)

	Exports		Imports		Total[a]	
	1998–2000	2008–10	1998–2000	2008–10	1998–2000	2008–10
With EU links	17.0	59.6	34.8	109.1	51.7	168.7
Egypt, Arab Rep.	3.8	25.5	15.5	50.2	19.3	75.7
Morocco	7.4	17.4	10.9	36.9	18.2	54.2
Tunisia	5.8	16.7	8.4	22.0	14.2	38.7
Memorandum items						
Arab League	174.8	751.5	153.9	565.4	328.7	1266.7
Mashreq	24.1	71.9	26.9	50.3	51.0	72.0
Mashreq w/Egypt, Arab Rep.	27.9	97.4	42.4	100.5	70.2	147.7
Maghreb Arab Union	28.3	95.8	28.9	100.3	57.2	196.1
World (trillion US$)	5.35	13.25	5.71	13.97	11.06	27.22
MENA share of world trade (%)	3.6	6.2	2.9	4.3	3.3	5.1

Source: World Integrated Trade Solution.
Note: — = Data not available or negligible.
a. Data may not add up horizontally (exports + imports) and are an underestimate because of missing and partial information.

Table C.4 Country's Share of MENA Total Trade with World (Annual Average %)

	Exports		Imports		Total[a]	
	1998–2000	2008–10	1998–2000	2008–10	1998–2000	2008–10
MENA region	100.0	100.0	100.0	100.0	100.0	100.0
Oil exporters	90.3	91.6	72.7	76.6	82.2	84.7
GCC	59.0	65.8	47.1	56.5	53.5	64.1
Bahrain	3.0	0.7	2.8	2.3	2.9	1.4
Kuwait	7.0	8.0	4.7	3.5	6.0	6.3
Oman	4.1	3.3	3.1	3.2	3.6	3.4
Qatar	3.5	5.8	1.8	4.1	2.8	5.3
Saudi Arabia	28.6	29.9	17.8	17.4	23.6	25.5
United Arab Emirates	12.9	18.1	16.9	25.9	14.7	22.2
Developing oil exporters	31.3	25.8	25.6	20.1	28.7	20.6
Algeria	7.6	7.3	5.6	6.6	6.7	7.3
Iran, Islamic Rep.	10.6	10.2	8.2	9.0	9.5	10.0
Iraq	8.6	6.1	7.4	—	8.1	—
Libya	—	—	—	—	—	—
Syrian Arab Republic	2.8	1.5	2.6	3.0	2.7	2.2
Yemen, Rep.	1.7	0.8	1.8	1.6	1.7	1.1
Oil importers	9.7	8.4	27.3	23.4	17.8	15.3
With GCC links	1.0	1.2	6.2	5.4	3.4	3.1
Djibouti	0.0	0.0	—	0.1	—	0.1
Jordan	0.7	0.7	2.3	2.5	1.4	1.5
Lebanon	0.4	0.5	3.9	2.8	2.0	1.5

(continued next page)

Table C.4 *(continued)*

	Exports		Imports		Total[a]	
	1998–2000	2008–10	1998–2000	2008–10	1998–2000	2008–10
With EU links	8.7	7.2	21.0	18.0	14.4	12.2
Egypt, Arab Rep.	2.0	3.1	9.4	8.3	5.4	5.5
Morocco	3.8	2.1	6.6	6.1	5.1	3.9
Tunisia	3.0	2.0	5.1	3.6	4.0	2.8
Memorandum items						
Arab League	90.0	91.1	93.1	93.2	91.4	91.7
Mashreq	12.4	8.7	16.3	8.3	14.2	5.2
Mashreq w/Egypt, Arab Rep.	14.4	11.8	25.6	16.6	19.5	10.7
Maghreb Arab Union	14.6	11.6	17.5	16.5	15.9	14.2

Source: World Integrated Trade Solution.

Note: — = Data not available or negligible.

a. Data may not add up horizontally (exports + imports) and are an underestimate because of missing and partial information.

Table C.5 Total MENA Trade in Goods with World (Annual Average, % of GDP)

	Exports		Imports		Total[a]	
	1998–2000	2008–10	1998–2000	2008–10	1998–2000	2008–10
MENA region	23.7	38.2	20.2	28.1	44.0	63.9
Oil exporters	33.8	44.2	23.2	27.2	57.1	68.4
GCC	39.3	55.2	26.7	34.9	66.1	90.1
Bahrain	83.3	27.2	67.1	65.6	150.5	92.8
Kuwait	43.5	51.0	24.9	16.4	68.4	67.4
Oman	47.5	50.4	31.0	36.6	78.5	87.0
Qatar	51.0	45.9	22.7	23.8	73.7	69.7
Saudi Arabia	33.6	57.6	17.8	24.7	51.5	82.4
United Arab Emirates	43.0	60.7	48.0	64.0	91.0	124.7
Developing oil exporters	31.0	32.7	21.6	18.7	52.6	43.8
Algeria	29.3	38.5	18.3	25.4	47.6	64.0
Iran, Islamic Rep.	20.0	25.0	13.1	16.3	33.1	41.4
Iraq	92.4	64.3	67.9	—	160.3	—
Libya	—	—	—	—	—	—
Syrian Arab Republic	32.2	22.2	25.5	32.8	57.7	55.0
Yemen, Rep.	42.0	24.2	39.1	35.3	81.1	59.5
Oil importers	10.6	17.8	25.3	36.6	36.0	54.4
With GCC links	7.5	15.8	39.7	53.9	47.3	69.7
Djibouti	0.0	15.5	—	63.8	—	79.3
Jordan	15.5	22.8	47.0	61.3	62.5	84.1
Lebanon	4.0	10.8	37.5	48.3	41.5	59.1

(continued next page)

Table C.5 *(continued)*

	Exports		Imports		Total[a]	
	1998–2000	*2008–10*	*1998–2000*	*2008–10*	*1998–2000*	*2008–10*
With EU links						
Egypt, Arab Rep.	11.2	18.4	23.1	33.7	34.3	52.1
Morocco	4.1	13.4	16.9	26.4	21.0	39.8
Tunisia	18.9	19.2	27.9	40.7	46.8	59.9
	28.9	0.4	42.0	51.3	71.0	90.3
Memorandum items						
Arab League	28.9	41.2	25.5	31.0	54.4	69.5
Mashreq	39.9	37.3	44.6	26.1	84.5	37.3
Mashreq w/Egypt, Arab Rep.	18.3	25.4	27.8	26.2	46.2	38.5
Maghreb Arab Union	20.0	25.8	20.5	27.0	40.5	52.8

Source: World Integrated Trade Solution. GDP data is sourced from the World Bank World Development Indicator database.

Note: — = Data not available or negligible.

a. Data may not add up horizontally (exports + imports) and are an underestimate because of missing and partial information.

Table C.6 Total Trade in Goods within MENA Region (Annual Average, US$ Billions)

	Exports		Imports		Total[a]	
	1998–2000	2008–10	1998–2000	2008–10	1998–2000	2008–10
MENA region	10.5	64.4	15.9	78.5	26.4	142.7
Oil exporters	8.4	50.2	11.7	57.7	20.1	107.7
GCC	5.8	33.7	7.9	34.5	13.8	68.2
Bahrain	0.6	1.8	0.5	1.2	1.1	3.0
Kuwait	0.4	1.1	1.1	3.3	1.5	4.4
Oman	1.3	2.5	1.7	6.5	3.0	9.0
Qatar	0.5	2.2	0.6	4.2	1.1	6.4
Saudi Arabia	2.6	20.5	2.0	8.7	4.6	29.2
United Arab Emirates	0.5	5.6	2.1	10.5	2.6	16.1
Developing oil exporters	2.6	16.5	3.7	23.2	6.3	39.5
Algeria	0.2	1.9	0.2	1.5	0.4	3.5
Iran, Islamic Rep.	1.0	9.2	1.1	16.5	2.1	25.7
Iraq	0.2	0.2	0.7	—	0.9	—
Libya	—	—	—	—	—	—
Syrian Arab Republic	1.0	4.4	0.5	2.6	1.5	7.0
Yemen, Rep.	0.2	0.8	1.2	2.5	1.5	3.3
Oil importers	2.1	14.2	4.2	20.8	6.3	35.0
With GCC links	0.8	4.4	1.3	7.5	2.2	11.8
Djibouti	—	0.0	—	0.2	—	0.2
Jordan	0.5	2.6	0.7	5.1	1.2	7.8
Lebanon	0.3	1.7	0.7	2.1	1.0	3.8

(continued next page)

Table C.6 *(continued)*

	Exports		Imports		Total[a]	
	1998–2000	2008–10	1998–2000	2008–10	1998–2000	2008–10
With EU links						
	1.3	9.8	2.8	13.3	4.1	23.2
Egypt, Arab Rep.	0.5	7.2	1.1	6.2	1.6	13.4
Morocco	0.3	0.8	1.2	5.2	1.5	5.9
Tunisia	0.4	1.9	0.5	2.0	1.0	3.9
Memorandum items						
Arab League	9.6	55.1	14.8	62.0	24.3	117.0
Mashreq	2.0	8.9	2.5	9.9	4.5	18.7
Mashreq w/Egypt Arab Rep.	2.5	16.1	3.6	16.1	6.1	32.0
Maghreb Arab Union	1.0	4.6	2.0	8.6	2.9	13.2

Source: World Integrated Trade Solution (WITS).

Note: — = Data not available or negligible. N.B. Due to missing data, in some cases the time period was adjusted to provide a three-year average. Notable adjustments include: Data are not available for Libya for the two time periods considered; Saudi Arabia's second time period exports with the MENA region and subregions is 2005–07; Iraq import data are only available for 2000 to 2002; Djibouti data are only available for 2009.

a. Data may not add up horizontally (exports + imports) and are an underestimate because of missing and partial information.

Table C.7 Total Trade in Goods within MENA Region (Annual Average, % of Total Trade)

	Exports		Imports		Total[a]	
	1998–2000	2008–10	1998–2000	2008–10	1998–2000	2008–10
MENA region	5.4	7.8	9.6	12.9	7.3	10.3
Oil exporters	4.8	6.6	9.7	12.4	6.8	9.2
GCC	5.1	6.2	10.2	10.1	7.2	7.7
Bahrain	9.8	31.2	11.1	8.7	10.4	15.3
Kuwait	2.8	1.6	14.6	15.8	7.1	5.1
Oman	16.3	9.3	33.0	33.1	22.9	19.3
Qatar	7.4	4.6	18.2	16.9	10.7	8.8
Saudi Arabia	4.7	8.3	6.6	8.3	5.4	8.3
United Arab Emirates	2.0	3.8	7.5	6.7	4.9	5.3
Developing oil exporters	4.3	7.7	8.8	19.0	6.1	13.9
Algeria	1.5	3.2	2.5	3.8	1.8	3.4
Iran, Islamic Rep.	4.7	11.0	8.0	30.1	6.0	18.5
Iraq	1.4	0.3	5.3	—	3.1	—
Libya	—	—	—	—	—	—
Syrian Arab Republic	17.8	36.0	12.0	14.5	15.2	23.2
Yemen, Rep.	6.5	12.4	41.0	27.0	23.1	21.1
Oil importers	11.0	20.5	9.3	14.7	9.8	16.6
With GCC links	42.5	45.3	12.9	22.8	17.6	27.9
Djibouti	—	24.5	—	31.4	—	30.1
Jordan	40.8	46.3	17.7	33.3	23.4	36.8
Lebanon	45.6	44.8	10.1	12.8	13.5	18.6

(continued next page)

Table C.7 *(continued)*

	Exports		Imports		Total[a]	
	1998–2000	2008–10	1998–2000	2008–10	1998–2000	2008–10
With EU links						
Egypt, Arab Rep.	7.4	16.5	8.2	12.2	7.9	13.7
Morocco	13.3	28.1	7.1	12.4	8.3	17.7
Tunisia	4.2	4.4	11.3	14.0	8.4	10.9
	7.6	11.4	6.2	8.9	6.8	10.0
Memorandum items						
Arab League	5.5	7.3	9.6	11.0	7.4	9.2
Mashreq	8.4	12.4	9.3	19.7	8.9	25.9
Mashreq w/Egypt, Arab Rep.	9.1	16.5	8.5	16.1	8.7	21.7
Maghreb Arab Union	3.4	4.8	6.8	8.6	5.1	6.7

Source: World Integrated Trade Solution.

Note: — = Data not available or negligible.

a. Data may not add up horizontally (exports + imports) and are an underestimate because of missing and partial information.

Table C.8　Country's Share of MENA Total Trade within MENA (Annual Average)

	Exports			Imports			Total[a]		
	1998–2000	2008–10		1998–2000	2008–10		1998–2000	2008–10	
MENA region	100.0	100.0		100.0	100.0		100.0	100.0	
Oil exporters	80.2	78.0		73.6	73.5		76.2	75.5	
GCC	55.5	52.3		50.1	44.0		52.3	47.8	
Bahrain	5.4	2.8		3.3	1.5		4.1	2.1	
Kuwait	3.7	1.6		7.2	4.3		5.8	3.1	
Oman	12.2	3.9		10.7	8.3		11.3	6.3	
Qatar	4.8	3.5		3.5	5.4		4.0	4.5	
Saudi Arabia	24.7	31.8		12.3	11.1		17.3	20.5	
United Arab Emirates	4.8	8.7		13.2	13.4		9.8	11.3	
Developing oil exporters	24.7	25.7		23.5	29.5		23.9	27.7	
Algeria	2.1	3.0		1.4	1.9		1.7	2.4	
Iran, Islamic Rep.	9.2	14.3		6.8	21.0		7.8	18.0	
Iraq	2.3	0.2		4.1	—		3.4	—	
Libya	—	—		—	—		—	—	
Syrian Arab Republic	9.2	6.9		3.2	3.4		5.6	4.9	
Yemen, Rep.	2.0	1.2		7.8	3.2		5.5	2.3	
Oil importers	19.8	22.0		26.4	26.5		23.8	24.5	
With GCC links	7.9	6.8		8.4	9.5		8.2	8.3	
Djibouti	—	0.1		—	0.3		—	0.2	
Jordan	4.9	4.1		4.3	6.5		4.5	5.5	
Lebanon	3.0	2.6		4.2	2.7		3.7	2.7	

(continued next page)

Table C.8 *(continued)*

	Exports		Imports		Total[a]	
	1998–2000	*2008–10*	*1998–2000*	*2008–10*	*1998–2000*	*2008–10*
With EU links						
	11.9	15.3	18.0	17.0	15.5	16.2
Egypt, Arab Rep.	4.8	11.1	6.9	7.9	6.1	9.4
Morocco	2.9	1.2	7.8	6.6	5.8	4.2
Tunisia	4.2	3.0	3.3	2.5	3.7	2.7
Memorandum items						
Arab League	90.8	85.7	93.2	79.0	92.2	82.0
Mashreq	19.3	13.8	15.8	12.6	17.2	13.1
Mashreq w/Egypt, Arab Rep.	24.1	24.9	22.7	20.6	23.3	22.5
Maghreb Arab Union	9.2	7.1	12.5	11.0	11.2	9.3

Source: World Integrated Trade Solution.

Note: — = Data not available or negligible.

a. Data may not add up horizontally (exports + imports) and are an underestimate because of missing and partial information.

Table C.9 Total MENA Trade in Goods within MENA (Annual Average, % of GDP)

	Exports		Imports		Total[a]	
	1998–2000	2008–10	1998–2000	2008–10	1998–2000	2008–10
MENA region	1.3	3.0	1.9	3.6	3.2	6.6
Oil exporters	1.6	2.9	2.3	3.4	3.9	6.3
GCC	2.0	3.4	2.7	3.5	4.7	6.9
Bahrain	8.2	8.5	7.5	5.7	15.7	14.2
Kuwait	1.2	0.8	3.6	2.6	4.9	3.4
Oman	7.7	4.7	10.2	12.1	18.0	16.8
Qatar	3.8	2.1	4.1	4.0	7.9	6.2
Saudi Arabia	1.6	4.8	1.2	2.0	2.8	6.8
United Arab Emirates	0.9	2.3	3.6	4.3	4.5	6.6
Developing oil exporters	1.3	2.5	1.9	3.6	3.2	6.1
Algeria	0.4	1.2	0.4	1.0	0.9	2.2
Iran, Islamic Rep.	0.9	2.8	1.1	4.9	2.0	7.7
Iraq	1.3	0.2	3.6	—	4.9	—
Libya	—	—	—	—	—	—
Syrian Arab Republic	5.7	8.0	3.1	4.8	8.8	12.8
Yemen, Rep.	2.7	3.0	16.0	9.6	18.8	12.6
Oil importers	1.2	3.7	2.4	5.4	3.5	9.0
With GCC links	3.2	7.2	5.1	12.3	8.3	19.5
Djibouti	—	3.8	—	20.0	—	23.9
Jordan	6.3	10.5	8.3	20.4	14.6	31.0
Lebanon	1.8	4.8	3.8	6.2	5.6	11.0

(continued next page)

Table C.9 *(continued)*

	Exports		Imports		Total[a]	
	1998–2000	*2008–10*	*1998–2000*	*2008–10*	*1998–2000*	*2008–10*
With EU links						
Egypt, Arab Rep.	0.8	3.0	1.9	4.1	2.7	7.2
Morocco	0.5	3.8	1.2	3.3	1.7	7.0
Tunisia	0.8	0.8	3.2	5.7	3.9	6.5
	2.2	4.4	2.6	4.6	4.8	9.0
Memorandum items						
Arab League	1.6	3.0	2.4	3.4	4.0	6.4
Mashreq	3.4	4.6	4.1	5.1	7.5	9.7
Mashreq w/Egypt, Arab Rep.	1.7	4.2	2.4	4.2	4.0	8.4
Maghreb Arab Union	0.7	1.2	1.4	2.3	2.1	3.6

Source: World Integrated Trade Solution. GDP data is sourced from the World Bank World Development Indicator database.

Note: — = Data not available or negligible.

a. Data may not add up horizontally (exports + imports) and are an underestimate because of missing and partial information.

Table C.10 MENA Trade with Other Regions (US$ Billions)

	EU27						United States					
	1995			2007			1995			2007		
	Export	Import	Total	Export	Import	Total	Export	Import	Total	Export	Import	Total
MENA	23.6	40.3	63.9	78.7	137.1	215.8	10.7	13.2	23.9	63.2	37.1	100.3
Oil exporters	14.5	23.2	37.7	50.8	94.2	145.0	9.9	9.7	19.6	60.5	30.1	90.6
GCC	8.3	16.6	24.9	19.5	75.1	94.6	8.3	8.3	16.6	41.9	27.0	68.9
Developing oil exporters	6.2	6.6	12.8	31.3	19.1	50.5	1.6	1.4	3.0	18.6	3.1	21.7
Oil importers	9.1	17.1	26.2	27.9	42.9	70.8	0.8	3.5	4.3	2.8	6.9	9.7
GCC links	0.1	1.3	1.4	0.6	7.9	8.5	0.0	0.3	0.4	1.3	1.8	3.1
EU links	9.0	15.8	24.8	27.3	35.0	62.3	0.8	3.2	3.9	1.4	5.1	6.6

	China						India					
	1995			2007			1995			2007		
	Export	Import	Total	Export	Import	Total	Export	Import	Total	Export	Import	Total
MENA	1.0	1.9	2.9	12.7	36.6	49.3	1.4	1.3	2.7	15.9	20.8	36.7
Oil exporters	0.9	1.3	2.2	12.3	30.1	42.4	0.7	1.0	1.8	12.9	19.3	32.2
GCC	0.9	1.1	2.0	9.9	25.8	35.7	0.7	1.0	1.8	10.3	18.1	28.4
Developing oil exporters	0.0	0.3	0.3	2.4	4.3	6.8	0.0	0.0	0.0	2.6	1.2	3.8
Oil importers	0.1	0.6	0.7	0.4	6.5	6.9	0.6	0.3	0.9	3.0	1.5	4.5
GCC links	0.0	0.1	0.1	0.1	2.3	2.5	0.2	0.1	0.2	0.5	0.5	1.0
EU links	0.1	0.5	0.6	0.3	4.1	4.4	0.5	0.2	0.7	2.5	1.0	3.5

(continued next page)

Table C.10 *(continued)*

| | MERCOSUR | | | | | | ASEAN | | | | | |
| | 1995 | | | 2007 | | | 1995 | | | 2007 | | |
	Export	Import	Total	Export	Import	Total	Export	Import	Total	Export	Import	Total
MENA	0.4	1.7	2.1	3.0	10.2	13.2	2.0	2.9	4.9	18.3	18.6	36.9
Oil exporters	0.3	0.9	1.2	2.3	6.8	9.0	1.8	2.2	3.9	17.8	16.5	34.3
GCC	0.0	0.7	0.7	0.3	4.6	4.9	1.7	2.0	3.7	16.0	15.1	31.1
Developing oil exporters	0.3	0.2	0.5	2.0	2.2	4.2	0.0	0.2	0.3	1.8	1.4	3.2
Oil importers	0.1	0.8	0.9	0.7	3.5	4.2	0.3	0.7	1.0	0.4	2.1	2.6
GCC links	0.0	0.1	0.1	0.0	0.6	0.6	0.1	0.2	0.3	0.1	0.8	0.9
EU links	0.1	0.7	0.8	0.7	2.9	3.6	0.2	0.5	0.7	0.3	1.3	1.6

Source: World Integrated Trade Solution.

Table C.11 MENA Trade with Other Regions (% of Total Flow with World)

	EU27						United States					
	1995			2007			1995			2007		
	Export	Import	Total	Export	Import	Total	Export	Import	Total	Export	Import	Total
MENA	19.9	34.5	27.2	10.9	28.3	17.8	9.0	11.3	10.1	8.7	7.7	8.3
Oil exporters	12.3	19.9	16.0	7.6	24.7	13.8	9.7	12.5	10.9	9.0	7.9	8.6
GCC	7.0	14.2	10.6	4.0	25.9	12.1	11.1	15.7	13.0	8.6	9.3	8.8
Developing oil exporters	5.3	5.6	5.4	17.2	20.9	18.4	5.6	5.7	5.7	10.2	3.4	7.9
Oil importers	7.7	14.6	11.1	52.4	41.6	45.3	4.9	8.9	7.8	5.2	6.7	6.2
GCC links	0.1	1.1	0.6	8.5	31.0	26.0	1.0	3.1	2.8	17.8	7.0	9.4
EU links	7.6	13.5	10.5	59.4	45.0	50.4	5.5	11.2	9.4	3.2	6.6	5.3

	China						India					
	1995			2007			1995			2007		
	Export	Import	Total	Export	Import	Total	Export	Import	Total	Export	Import	Total
MENA	0.9	1.7	1.2	1.7	7.6	4.1	1.2	1.1	1.1	2.2	4.3	3.0
Oil exporters	0.9	1.7	1.2	1.8	7.9	4.0	0.7	1.3	1.0	1.9	5.1	3.1
GCC	1.2	2.0	1.6	2.0	8.9	4.6	1.0	2.0	1.4	2.1	6.3	3.6
Developing oil exporters	0.0	1.0	0.5	1.3	4.7	2.5	0.0	0.1	0.0	1.4	1.3	1.4
Oil importers	0.6	1.5	1.3	0.7	6.3	4.4	4.0	0.7	1.6	5.6	1.4	2.9
GCC links	0.9	0.8	0.8	1.8	9.2	7.5	7.8	0.6	1.8	6.6	1.9	2.9
EU links	0.6	1.8	1.4	0.6	5.3	3.6	3.4	0.7	1.6	5.5	1.3	2.9

(continued next page)

Table C.11 *(continued)*

	MERCOSUR						ASEAN					
	1995			*2007*			*1995*			*2007*		
	Export	*Import*	*Total*	*Export*	*Import*	*Total*	*Export*	*Import*	*Total*	*Export*	*Import*	*Total*
MENA	0.3	1.5	0.9	0.4	2.1	1.1	1.7	2.5	2.1	2.5	3.8	3.0
Oil exporters	0.3	1.2	0.7	0.3	1.8	0.9	1.7	2.8	2.2	2.7	4.3	3.3
GCC	0.0	1.4	0.6	0.1	1.6	0.6	2.3	3.7	2.9	3.3	5.2	4.0
Developing oil exporters	0.9	0.8	0.9	1.1	2.4	1.5	0.2	0.8	0.5	1.0	1.5	1.2
Oil importers	0.6	2.0	1.6	1.4	3.4	2.7	1.6	1.9	1.8	0.8	2.1	1.6
GCC links	0.3	0.9	0.8	0.3	2.2	1.8	4.3	1.9	2.2	1.7	3.2	2.9
EU links	0.6	2.4	1.8	1.5	3.7	2.9	1.2	1.9	1.7	0.7	1.7	1.3

Source: World Integrated Trade Solution.

Table C.12 MENA Trade with Other Regions (% of GDP)

	EU27						United States					
	1995			2007			1995			2007		
	Export	Import	Total	Export	Import	Total	Export	Import	Total	Export	Import	Total
MENA	4.2	7.1	11.3	4.4	7.6	12.0	1.9	2.3	4.2	3.5	2.1	5.6
Oil exporters	3.3	5.3	8.6	3.4	6.2	9.6	2.3	2.2	4.5	4.0	2.0	6.0
GCC	3.1	6.3	9.5	2.2	8.4	10.5	3.2	3.1	6.3	4.7	3.0	7.7
Developing oil exporters	3.6	3.8	7.4	5.1	3.1	8.2	0.9	0.8	1.7	3.0	0.5	3.5
Oil importers	7.0	13.1	20.1	9.7	14.9	24.6	0.6	2.7	3.3	1.0	2.4	3.4
GCC links	0.5	6.9	7.4	1.4	18.0	19.4	0.1	1.8	1.9	3.0	4.1	7.0
EU links	8.1	14.2	22.3	11.2	14.3	25.5	0.7	2.9	3.5	0.6	2.1	2.7

	China						India					
	1995			2007			1995			2007		
	Export	Import	Total	Export	Import	Total	Export	Import	Total	Export	Import	Total
MENA	0.2	0.3	0.5	0.7	2.0	2.7	0.2	0.2	0.5	0.9	1.2	2.0
Oil exporters	0.2	0.3	0.5	0.8	2.0	2.8	0.2	0.2	0.4	0.9	1.3	2.1
GCC	0.3	0.4	0.8	1.1	2.9	4.0	0.3	0.4	0.7	1.1	2.0	3.2
Developing oil exporters	0.0	0.1	0.2	0.4	0.7	1.1	0.0	0.0	0.0	0.4	0.2	0.6
Oil importers	0.1	0.5	0.5	0.1	2.2	2.4	0.5	0.2	0.7	1.0	0.5	1.6
GCC links	0.1	0.4	0.5	0.3	5.3	5.6	0.9	0.4	1.2	1.1	1.1	2.2
EU links	0.1	0.5	0.5	0.1	1.7	1.8	0.4	0.2	0.6	1.0	0.4	1.4

(continued next page)

Table C.12 *(continued)*

	MERCOSUR						ASEAN					
	1995			2007			1995			2007		
	Export	Import	Total	Export	Import	Total	Export	Import	Total	Export	Import	Total
MENA	0.1	0.3	0.4	0.2	0.6	0.7	0.4	0.5	0.9	1.0	1.0	2.0
Oil exporters	0.1	0.2	0.3	0.1	0.4	0.6	0.4	0.5	0.9	1.2	1.1	2.3
GCC	0.0	0.3	0.3	0.0	0.5	0.5	0.6	0.7	1.4	1.8	1.7	3.5
Developing oil exporters	0.1	0.1	0.3	0.3	0.4	0.7	0.0	0.1	0.1	0.3	0.2	0.5
Oil importers	0.1	0.6	0.7	0.3	1.2	1.5	0.2	0.6	0.8	0.2	0.7	0.9
GCC links	0.0	0.5	0.6	0.1	1.3	1.3	0.5	1.1	1.6	0.3	1.9	2.1
EU links	0.1	0.6	0.7	0.3	1.2	1.5	0.1	0.5	0.6	0.1	0.5	0.7

Source: World Integrated Trade Solution.

Table C.13 Intraregional Trade Comparison

	Exports		Imports		Total[a]	
	1998–2000	2008–10	1998–2000	2008–10	1998–2000	2008–10
Annual average, US$ billions						
MENA	10.5	64.4	15.9	78.5	26.4	142.7
Oil exporters with MENA	8.4	50.2	11.7	57.7	20.1	107.7
Oil importers with MENA	2.1	14.2	4.2	20.8	6.3	35.0
Arab League	9.6	55.1	14.8	62.0	24.3	117.0
All high-income (OECD plus non-OECD)	3025.0	5518.4	3095.3	5567.8	6120.3	11086.1
ASEAN	80.6	228.5	80.6	228.5	161.2	457.0
EU27	1552.0	3355.2	1552.0	3355.2	3104.0	6710.4
Low and middle income economies	227.8	1292.9	227.8	1292.9	455.5	2585.8
MERCOSUR	19.7	45.3	19.7	45.3	39.4	90.5
NAFTA	568.3	829.3	568.3	829.3	1136.6	1658.5
Annual average, % of trade flow						
MENA	5.4	7.8	9.6	12.9	7.3	10.3
Oil exporters with MENA	4.8	6.6	9.7	12.4	6.8	9.2
Oil importers with MENA	11.0	20.5	9.3	14.7	9.8	16.6
Arab League	5.5	7.3	9.6	11.0	7.4	9.2
All high-income (OECD plus non-OECD)	75.2	66.5	69.9	59.2	72.4	62.6
ASEAN	22.0	25.2	25.9	27.4	23.8	26.3
EU27	67.4	65.6	67.3	63.8	67.3	64.7

(continued next page)

Table C.13 *(continued)*

	Exports		Imports		Total[a]	
	1998–2000	2008–10	1998–2000	2008–10	1998–2000	2008–10
Low and middle income economies	20.8	30.9	21.8	33.3	21.3	32.1
MERCOSUR	19.2	14.0	19.1	17.1	19.1	15.4
NAFTA	54.3	48.5	39.1	32.4	45.4	38.8
Annual average, % of GDP						
MENA	1.3	3.0	1.9	3.6	3.2	6.6
Oil exporters with MENA	1.6	2.9	2.3	3.4	3.9	6.3
Oil importers with MENA	1.2	3.7	2.4	5.4	3.5	9.0
Arab League	1.6	3.0	2.4	3.4	4.0	6.4
All high-income (OECD plus non-OECD)	11.8	12.9	12.1	13.0	23.9	25.9
ASEAN	14.9	14.4	14.9	14.4	29.9	28.8
EU27	17.4	19.8	17.4	19.8	34.8	39.6
Low and middle income economies	4.1	7.2	4.1	7.2	8.1	14.4
MERCOSUR	1.9	2.1	1.9	2.1	3.9	4.2
NAFTA	5.7	5.3	5.7	5.3	11.4	10.5

Sources: World Integrated Trade Solution (WITS); WTO International Trade Statistics; World Development Indicators (WDI) for current GDP (US$) figures.
a. Data may not add up horizontally (exports + imports) and are an underestimate because of missing and partial information.

146

Table C.14 MENA Nonfuel Trade with World (Annual Average, US$ Billions)

	Exports		Imports		Total[a]	
	1998–2000	2008–10	1998–2000	2008–10	1998–2000	2008–10
MENA region	36.0	204.0	155.4	569.7	191.5	773.6
Oil exporters	19.2	146.7	114.3	451.6	133.6	598.2
GCC	14.4	111.8	75.1	339.3	89.4	451.1
Bahrain	3.2	3.4	3.5	9.3	6.7	12.8
Kuwait	1.1	3.2	7.8	24.7	8.8	27.9
Oman	1.8	8.2	5.1	18.7	6.8	26.9
Qatar	0.7	27.0	3.0	25.4	3.7	52.4
Saudi Arabia	5.7	68.8	29.4	105.8	35.1	174.6
United Arab Emirates	1.8	1.1	26.3	155.5	28.2	156.5
Developing oil exporters	4.9	34.9	39.3	112.3	44.1	147.1
Algeria	0.4	1.1	9.1	39.3	9.5	40.4
Iran, Islamic Rep.	2.8	24.5	13.3	53.2	16.1	77.7
Iraq	0.6	0.1	13.2	—	13.8	—
Libya	—	—	—	—	—	—
Syrian Arab Republic	1.1	8.8	3.7	12.4	4.8	21.2
Yemen, Rep.	—	0.4	—	7.4	—	7.8

(continued next page)

Table C.14 *(continued)*

	Exports		Imports		Total[a]	
	1998–2000	*2008–10*	*1998–2000*	*2008–10*	*1998–2000*	*2008–10*
Oil importers	16.8	57.3	41.1	118.1	57.9	175.4
With GCC links	2.0	9.6	9.3	25.9	11.3	35.5
Djibouti	—	0.1	—	0.6	—	0.8
Jordan	1.3	5.7	3.5	12.2	4.8	17.9
Lebanon	0.7	3.7	5.8	13.1	6.5	16.8
With EU links	14.9	47.8	31.8	92.1	46.6	139.9
Egypt, Arab Rep.	2.4	16.8	14.5	44.4	16.9	61.3
Morocco	7.2	16.7	9.4	28.8	16.6	45.5
Tunisia	5.3	14.2	7.8	18.9	13.1	33.1
World (Trillion US$)	4.92	11.27	5.24	11.74	10.16	23.01
MENA share of world trade (%)	0.7	1.8	3.0	4.9	1.9	3.4

Source: World Integrated Trade Solution.
Note: — = Data not available or negligible.
a. Data may not add up horizontally (exports + imports) and are an underestimate because of missing and partial information.

Table C.15   MENA Nonfuel Trade with World (Annual Average, % of Total Trade)

	Exports		Imports		Total[a]	
	1998–2000	2008–10	1998–2000	2008–10	1998–2000	2008–10
MENA region	18.6	24.7	94.0	93.9	53.2	56.0
Oil exporters	11.0	19.4	95.1	97.2	45.2	51.1
GCC	12.5	20.6	96.3	99.0	46.5	51.0
Bahrain	55.9	59.7	75.6	67.1	64.7	64.9
Kuwait	8.0	4.9	99.4	116.8	41.3	32.1
Oman	22.6	30.5	98.7	95.1	52.6	57.7
Qatar	10.4	56.3	99.5	102.1	37.8	71.9
Saudi Arabia	10.3	27.9	99.8	99.9	41.3	49.5
United Arab Emirates	7.3	0.7	94.4	98.8	53.3	51.0
Developing oil exporters	8.0	16.4	92.7	92.0	42.8	51.6
Algeria	2.4	1.8	98.5	98.5	39.4	40.2
Iran, Islamic Rep.	13.7	29.2	98.3	97.3	47.3	56.1
Iraq	3.6	0.3	107.5	—	47.6	—
Libya	—	—	—	—	—	—
Syrian Arab Republic	20.3	71.9	85.7	68.6	49.2	69.9
Yemen, Rep.	—	6.9	—	78.5	—	49.4
Oil importers	88.9	82.8	91.1	83.2	90.4	83.1
Oil importers with GCC links	99.9	99.4	90.1	79.0	91.7	83.7
Djibouti	—	93.5	—	93.5	—	93.5
Jordan	100.0	99.4	91.3	79.3	93.5	84.8
Lebanon	99.9	99.7	89.4	78.2	90.4	82.1
Oil importers with EU links	87.7	80.1	91.4	84.5	90.2	82.9
Egypt, Arab Rep.	63.1	66.0	93.9	88.5	87.8	80.9
Morocco	97.4	96.3	86.9	78.0	91.1	83.9
Tunisia	91.4	84.8	92.5	86.2	92.1	85.6

Source: World Integrated Trade Solution.
Note: — = Data not available or negligible.
a. Data may not add up horizontally (exports + imports) and are an underestimate because of missing and partial information.

Table C.16 MENA Nonfuel Trade with World (Annual Average, % of GDP)

	Exports		Imports		Total[a]	
	1998–2000	2008–10	1998–2000	2008–10	1998–2000	2008–10
MENA region	5.2	9.7	22.4	27.2	27.6	36.9
Oil exporters	3.7	8.6	22.1	26.4	25.8	35.0
GCC	4.9	11.4	25.8	34.5	30.7	45.9
Bahrain	46.6	16.2	50.7	44.0	97.3	60.2
Kuwait	3.5	2.5	24.8	19.1	28.3	21.6
Oman	10.7	15.3	30.6	34.8	41.3	50.1
Qatar	5.3	25.8	22.6	24.3	27.8	50.1
Saudi Arabia	3.5	16.1	17.8	24.7	21.3	40.8
United Arab Emirates	3.1	0.4	45.3	63.2	48.5	63.7
Developing oil exporters	2.1	4.8	17.3	15.4	19.5	20.2
Algeria	0.7	0.7	18.0	25.0	18.7	25.7
Iran, Islamic Rep.	2.7	7.3	12.9	15.9	15.6	23.2
Iraq	3.4	0.2	73.0	—	76.4	—
Libya	—	—	—	—	—	—
Syrian Arab Republic	6.5	16.0	21.9	22.5	28.4	38.5
Yemen, Rep.	—	1.7	—	27.7	—	29.4
Oil importers	9.5	14.9	23.2	30.7	32.7	45.6
Oil importers with GCC links	7.5	15.7	35.8	42.6	43.3	58.3
Djibouti	—	14.5	—	59.6	—	74.1
Jordan	15.5	22.6	42.9	48.7	58.4	71.3
Lebanon	4.0	10.7	33.6	37.8	37.5	48.5
Oil importers with EU links	9.9	14.8	21.1	28.5	30.9	43.2
Egypt, Arab Rep.	2.6	8.9	15.8	23.4	18.4	32.2
Morocco	18.4	18.5	24.3	31.8	42.7	50.3
Tunisia	26.5	33.1	38.9	44.2	65.3	77.2

Sources: World Integrated Trade Solution and World Bank.

Note: — = Data not available or negligible.

a. Data may not add up horizontally (exports + imports) and are an underestimate because of missing and partial information.

Table C.17 MENA Nonfuel Trade within MENA (Annual Average, US$ Billions)

	Exports		Imports		Total[a]	
	1998–2000	2008–10	1998–2000	2008–10	1998–2000	2008–10
MENA region	8.9	49.1	11.7	63.3	20.6	112.3
Oil exporters	6.9	35.7	9.8	54.0	16.6	89.6
GCC	5.4	20.0	7.6	33.3	13.0	53.3
Bahrain	0.5	2.2	0.5	1.3	0.9	3.5
Kuwait	0.4	1.1	1.1	3.4	1.5	4.5
Oman	1.2	1.9	1.6	5.9	2.9	7.8
Qatar	0.2	1.1	0.5	4.3	0.8	5.4
Saudi Arabia	2.6	8.3	1.9	8.7	4.6	17.0
United Arab Emirates	0.4	5.4	1.9	9.7	2.3	15.1
Developing oil exporters	1.5	15.8	2.2	20.7	3.6	36.3
Algeria	0.1	0.2	0.2	1.5	0.3	1.7
Iran, Islamic Rep.	0.6	7.6	1.1	16.2	1.6	23.8
Iraq	0.2	0.1	0.5	—	0.7	—
Libya	—	—	—	—	—	—
Syrian Arab Republic	0.6	7.6	0.4	2.1	1.0	9.7
Yemen, Rep.	—	0.3	—	0.9	—	1.2
Oil importers	2.1	13.4	2.0	9.2	4.0	22.6
With GCC links	0.8	4.3	0.8	4.1	1.6	8.4
Djibouti	—	0.0	—	0.2	—	0.2
Jordan	0.5	2.6	0.4	2.3	0.9	4.9
Lebanon	0.3	1.7	0.4	1.6	0.7	3.3
With EU links	1.2	9.1	1.2	5.2	2.4	14.3
Egypt, Arab Rep.	0.5	6.5	0.6	2.7	1.1	9.2
Morocco	0.3	0.7	0.3	1.7	0.6	2.5
Tunisia	0.4	1.9	0.3	0.7	0.7	2.6

Source: World Integrated Trade Solution.

Note: — = Data not available or negligible.

a. Data may not add up horizontally (exports + imports) and are an underestimate because of missing and partial information.

Table C.18 MENA Total Trade by Sector (Annual Average, US$ Billions)

	Exports		Imports		Total trade[a]	
	1998–2000	2008–10	1998–2000	2008–10	1998–2000	2008–10
Fuel Trade with World (SITC 3)						
MENA region	159.8	627.3	6.8	41.9	166.5	619.2
Oil exporters	157.7	615.4	2.7	18.1	160.4	583.4
GCC	102.2	434.9	2.2	7.8	104.4	442.7
Bahrain	4.1	4.7	1.8	4.6	5.9	9.3
Kuwait	12.5	64.8	0.0	0.1	12.6	65.0
Oman	6.1	22.4	0.1	1.0	6.2	23.3
Qatar	6.2	42.9	0.0	0.2	6.2	43.1
Saudi Arabia	49.8	219.5	0.1	0.1	49.8	219.6
United Arab Emirates	23.6	80.5	0.2	1.8	23.8	82.3
Developing oil exporters	55.5	180.5	0.5	10.2	56.0	140.7
Algeria	14.4	59.5	0.1	0.6	14.6	60.1
Iran, Islamic Rep.	17.7	59.3	0.2	1.5	18.0	60.8
Iraq	19.8	50.0	0.0	—	19.8	—
Libya	—	—	—	—	—	—
Syrian Arab Republic	3.5	5.5	0.1	5.7	3.7	11.2
Yemen, Rep.	—	6.2	—	2.5	—	8.6
Oil importers	2.1	11.9	4.0	23.8	6.1	35.7
With GCC links	0.0	0.1	1.0	6.9	1.0	6.9
Djibouti	—	0.0	—	0.0	—	0.1
Jordan	0.0	0.0	0.3	3.2	0.3	3.2
Lebanon	0.0	0.0	0.7	3.7	0.7	3.7
With EU links	2.1	11.9	3.0	16.9	5.1	28.8
Egypt, Arab Rep.	1.4	8.7	0.9	5.8	2.3	14.4

Morocco	0.2	0.6	1.4	8.1	1.6	8.8
Tunisia	0.5	2.5	0.6	3.0	1.1	5.6
Manufactures Trade with World (SITC 5, 6, 7, 8 minus SITC 68 (Non-Ferrous Metals)						
MENA region	23.8	94.1	104.9	385.6	128.6	479.6
Oil exporters	11.7	54.0	75.7	298.7	87.4	352.7
GCC	9.3	35.5	54.9	216.5	64.2	252.0
Bahrain	0.6	1.1	1.7	6.6	2.3	7.7
Kuwait	0.9	2.9	5.1	20.0	6.0	22.9
Oman	1.3	2.6	3.7	13.6	5.0	16.2
Qatar	0.7	2.5	2.6	22.2	3.3	24.7
Saudi Arabia	5.1	20.0	21.9	52.6	27.0	72.7
United Arab Emirates	0.6	6.3	20.0	101.5	20.6	107.8
Developing oil exporters	2.4	18.5	20.8	82.2	23.2	100.7
Algeria	0.3	0.6	6.1	30.9	6.4	31.5
Iran, Islamic Rep.	1.7	13.1	10.1	38.3	11.8	51.3
Iraq	0.1	0.0	2.1	—	2.2	—
Libya	—	—	—	—	—	—
Syrian Arab Republic	0.4	4.7	2.5	8.4	2.8	13.2
Yemen, Rep.	—	0.1	—	4.7	—	4.7
Oil importers	12.1	40.0	29.2	86.9	41.3	126.9
With GCC links	1.2	6.6	6.4	18.6	7.6	25.2
Djibouti	—	0.1	—	0.4	—	0.5
Jordan	0.8	4.2	2.4	8.8	3.2	12.9
Lebanon	0.4	2.2	3.9	9.5	4.4	11.7
With EU links	10.9	33.5	22.8	68.2	33.7	101.7
Egypt, Arab Rep.	1.5	10.2	9.0	30.7	10.5	40.8
Tunisia	4.6	12.4	6.6	15.4	11.2	27.8

(continued next page)

Table C.18 (*continued*)

	Exports		Imports		Total trade[a]	
	1998–2000	2008–10	1998–2000	2008–10	1998–2000	2008–10
Machinery & Transport Equipment Trade with World (SITC 7)						
MENA region	3.3	14.4	50.3	188.5	52.4	202.8
Oil exporters	1.5	5.1	37.8	150.5	38.0	155.6
GCC	1.4	2.9	27.3	113.5	28.7	116.3
Bahrain	0.0	0.2	0.7	3.6	0.8	3.8
Kuwait	0.1	0.2	2.5	10.1	2.6	10.3
Oman	0.9	0.4	2.2	7.8	3.1	8.2
Qatar	0.0	0.0	1.4	12.7	1.4	12.7
Saudi Arabia	0.3	1.0	11.3	32.1	11.5	33.1
United Arab Emirates	0.1	1.1	9.2	47.1	9.2	48.2
Developing oil exporters	0.1	2.2	10.4	37.0	9.4	39.2
Algeria	0.0	0.0	3.1	15.8	3.1	15.8
Iran, Islamic Rep.	0.1	1.5	5.3	16.8	5.4	18.4
Iraq	—	0.0	1.2	—	—	—
Libya	—	—	—	—	—	—
Syrian Arab Republic	0.0	0.7	0.8	2.1	0.8	2.7
Yemen, Rep.	—	0.0	—	2.3	—	2.3
Oil importers	1.7	9.3	12.6	38.0	14.3	47.3
With GCC links	0.2	1.1	2.7	7.9	2.9	9.0
Djibouti	—	0.1	—	0.2	—	0.3
Jordan	0.1	0.3	1.1	3.7	1.2	4.0
Lebanon	0.1	0.6	1.6	3.9	1.7	4.6
With EU links	1.6	8.2	9.9	30.1	11.4	38.3

154

Egypt, Arab Rep.	0.0	1.1	4.0	12.5	4.1	13.6
Morocco	0.7	3.0	3.1	10.6	3.9	13.5
Tunisia	0.8	4.1	2.7	7.0	3.5	11.1
Textiles Trade with World (26+65+84 of SITC Rev. 1)						
MENA region	8.5	14.8	11.7	21.4	20.2	36.2
Oil exporters	2.3	4.1	7.0	11.9	9.3	15.9
GCC	1.0	0.7	5.7	9.3	6.7	10.0
Bahrain	0.3	0.1	0.2	0.3	0.6	0.4
Kuwait	0.0	0.0	0.4	1.1	0.4	1.1
Oman	0.1	0.0	0.2	0.3	0.4	0.3
Qatar	0.1	0.0	0.2	0.5	0.3	0.5
Saudi Arabia	0.1	0.2	1.9	1.8	2.1	2.0
United Arab Emirates	0.2	0.3	2.8	5.2	3.0	5.5
Developing oil exporters	1.3	3.4	1.2	2.6	2.6	6.0
Algeria	0.0	0.0	0.2	0.5	0.2	0.5
Iran, Islamic Rep.	0.8	1.2	0.5	1.2	1.3	2.4
Iraq	0.0	0.0	0.1	—	0.1	—
Libyan Arab Jamahiriya	—	—	—	—	—	—
Syrian Arab Republic	0.5	2.2	0.4	0.7	0.9	2.9
Yemen, Rep.	—	0.0	—	0.2	—	0.2
Oil importers	6.2	10.7	4.7	9.5	10.9	20.3
With GCC links	0.2	1.1	0.6	1.6	0.8	2.7
Djibouti	—	0.0	—	0.0	—	0.0
Jordan	0.1	0.9	0.2	0.9	0.3	1.8
Lebanon	0.1	0.1	0.4	0.7	0.5	0.8

(continued next page)

Table C.18 *(continued)*

	Exports		Imports		Total trade[a]	
	1998–2000	*2008–10*	*1998–2000*	*2008–10*	*1998–2000*	*2008–10*
With EU links	6.0	9.7	4.1	7.9	10.1	17.6
Tunisia	2.5	3.8	1.9	2.6	4.4	6.4
Agriculture Trade with World (SITC 0+1+2-27-28+4)						
MENA region	6.2	24.7	27.8	81.3	33.9	105.9
Oil exporters	2.9	13.9	18.4	57.5	21.3	71.3
GCC	1.1	4.5	11.6	34.4	12.7	38.9
Bahrain	0.0	0.3	0.5	1.2	0.5	1.5
Kuwait	0.0	0.2	1.2	3.8	1.3	4.0
Oman	0.4	0.8	1.1	2.3	1.4	3.1
Qatar	0.0	0.0	0.4	2.0	0.4	2.0
Saudi Arabia	0.5	1.6	5.2	13.8	5.7	15.4
United Arab Emirates	0.2	1.7	3.2	11.2	3.3	12.9
Developing oil exporters	1.8	9.4	6.8	23.1	8.6	32.4
Algeria	0.0	0.2	2.9	7.8	2.9	8.0
Iran, Islamic Rep.	1.0	5.4	2.8	9.6	3.8	15.0
Iraq	0.2	0.0	0.2	—	0.4	—
Libya	—	—	—	—	—	—

Syrian Arab Republic	0.6	3.3	0.8	3.0	1.5	6.3
Yemen, Rep.	—	0.4	—	2.7	—	3.0
Oil importers	3.2	10.8	9.4	23.8	12.7	34.6
With GCC links	0.4	1.4	2.3	5.6	2.6	7.0
Djibouti	—	0.0	—	0.2	—	0.2
Jordan	0.2	0.9	0.9	2.8	1.1	3.7
Lebanon	0.1	0.5	1.3	2.7	1.5	3.2
With EU links	2.9	9.4	7.2	18.1	10.0	27.6
Egypt, Arab Rep.	0.6	4.3	4.3	10.6	4.9	14.9
Morocco	1.7	3.6	1.9	5.0	3.6	8.7
Tunisia	0.6	1.5	1.0	2.5	1.6	4.0

Source: World Integrated Trade Solution (WITS).

Note: — = Data not available or negligible.

a. Data may not add up horizontally (exports + imports) and are an underestimate because of missing and partial information.

Table C.19   MENA Trade by Sector (% of Trade Flow)

	Exports		Imports		Total trade[a]	
	1998–2000	2008–10	1998–2000	2008–10	1998–2000	2008–10
Fuel Trade with World (SITC 3)						
MENA region	80.2	76.0	3.0	6.9	44.7	44.8
Oil exporters						
GCC	85.6	80.2	0.6	2.3	51.2	50.0
Bahrain	71.1	81.6	1.2	32.9	0.6	47.2
Kuwait	92.0	98.4	0.6	0.7	58.7	74.7
Oman	77.4	82.7	1.3	4.9	47.4	50.0
Qatar	89.6	89.5	0.5	0.8	62.2	59.2
Saudi Arabia	89.7	89.0	0.2	0.1	58.7	62.3
United Arab Emirates	94.4	53.9	0.8	1.2	45.1	26.9
Developing oil exporters	91.4	84.7	1.2	8.4	54.3	49.4
Algeria	97.6	98.2	1.5	1.5	60.6	59.8
Iran, Islamic Rep.	86.3	70.8	1.7	2.7	52.7	43.9
Iraq	118.3	99.7	0.0	—	68.2	—
Libya	—	—	—	—	—	—
Syrian Arab Republic	65.4	45.2	3.3	31.4	38.0	37.0
Yemen, Rep.	—	95.7	—	26.3	—	54.5
Oil importers						
With GCC links	11.1	17.2	8.9	16.8	9.6	16.9
Djibouti	0.1	0.6	9.9	21.0	8.3	16.3
Jordan	—	6.5	—	6.5	—	6.5
Lebanon	0.0	0.6	8.7	20.7	6.5	15.2
With EU links	0.1	0.3	10.6	21.8	9.6	17.9
Egypt, Arab Rep.	12.3	19.9	8.6	15.5	9.8	17.1
	36.9	34.0	6.1	11.5	12.2	19.1

Morocco	2.6	3.7	13.1	22.0	16.1
Tunisia	8.6	15.2	7.5	13.8	14.4
Manufactures Trade with World					
MENA region	12.2	11.4	63.4	63.5	34.7
Oil exporters					
GCC	8.1	6.6	70.4	63.2	28.5
Bahrain	10.4	19.3	37.0	47.3	39.1
Kuwait	6.9	4.4	65.2	94.5	26.3
Oman	16.4	9.7	71.9	69.3	34.8
Qatar	10.2	5.2	83.7	89.1	33.9
Saudi Arabia	9.2	8.1	74.4	49.7	20.6
United Arab Emirates	2.6	4.2	71.6	64.5	35.2
Developing oil exporters	4.0	8.7	49.1	67.3	35.3
Algeria	1.7	0.9	66.2	77.4	31.3
Iran, Islamic Rep.	8.2	15.6	74.8	70.0	37.1
Iraq	0.6	0.1	17.0	—	—
Libya	—	—	—	—	—
Syrian Arab Republic	6.7	38.7	57.6	46.6	43.4
Yemen, Rep.	—	0.9	—	49.4	29.7
Oil importers	64.0	57.8	64.7	61.2	60.1
With GCC links	61.7	68.3	61.6	56.8	59.4
Djibouti	—	91.5	—	62.5	68.2
Jordan	59.6	73.0	63.3	56.9	61.3
Lebanon	65.5	60.2	60.6	56.5	57.2
With EU links	64.3	56.1	65.7	62.5	60.3
Egypt, Arab Rep.	39.6	39.9	57.9	61.1	53.9

(continued next page)

Table C.19 *(continued)*

Machinery & Transport Equipment Trade with World (SITC 7)

	Exports		Imports		Total trade[a]	
	1998–2000	2008–10	1998–2000	2008–10	1998–2000	2008–10
MENA region	1.7	1.7	30.4	31.1	14.6	14.7
Oil exporters						
GCC	1.2	0.5	35.0	33.1	14.9	13.1
Bahrain	0.7	2.7	16.0	26.0	7.5	19.2
Kuwait	0.8	0.3	32.4	47.9	12.3	11.8
Oman	11.2	1.5	43.8	39.7	24.1	17.6
Qatar	0.0	0.1	44.6	51.0	13.7	17.5
Saudi Arabia	0.5	0.4	38.3	30.3	13.6	9.4
United Arab Emirates	0.3	0.7	32.9	30.0	17.5	15.7
Developing oil exporters	0.2	1.0	24.7	30.3	9.1	13.8
Algeria	0.3	0.0	33.3	39.6	13.0	15.8
Iran, Islamic Rep.	0.5	1.8	39.5	30.8	15.9	13.3
Iraq	—	0.0	10.0	—	—	—
Libyan Arab Jamahiriya	—	—	—	—	—	—
Syrian Arab Republic	0.1	5.4	18.6	11.5	8.3	9.0
Yemen, Rep.	—	0.0	—	24.4	—	14.5
Oil importers	9.1	13.4	27.9	26.8	22.4	22.4
With GCC links	8.2	11.2	26.2	24.0	23.3	21.1
Djibouti	—	86.9	—	32.6	—	43.2
Jordan	6.1	5.5	29.6	24.2	23.8	19.2
Lebanon	12.1	16.8	24.2	23.5	23.0	22.3
With EU links	9.2	13.8	28.4	27.6	22.1	22.7
Egypt, Arab Rep.	0.9	4.4	26.0	24.9	21.0	18.0

Morocco	10.2	17.2	28.6	28.7	21.2	25.0
Tunisia	13.5	24.6	32.7	32.0	24.8	28.8
Textiles Trade with World (26+65+84 of SITC Rev.1)						
MENA region	4.4	1.8	7.1	3.5	5.6	2.6
Oil exporters						
GCC	0.9	0.1	7.3	2.7	3.5	1.1
Bahrain	5.8	2.3	5.1	2.2	5.5	2.2
Kuwait	0.1	0.0	5.4	5.2	2.0	1.3
Oman	1.8	0.1	4.2	1.6	2.7	0.7
Qatar	1.7	0.0	5.0	2.1	2.7	0.7
Saudi Arabia	0.3	0.1	6.5	1.7	2.4	0.6
United Arab Emirates	0.9	0.2	9.9	3.3	5.7	1.8
Developing oil exporters	2.2	1.6	2.9	2.1	2.5	2.1
Algeria	0.0	0.0	2.5	1.2	1.0	0.5
Iran, Islamic Rep.	4.0	1.4	3.7	2.3	3.9	1.8
Iraq	0.1	0.0	0.6	—	0.3	—
Libya	—	—	—	—	—	—
Syrian Arab Republic	9.0	17.6	10.2	4.0	9.5	9.5
Yemen, Rep.	—	0.0	—	1.6	—	1.0
Oil importers	32.8	15.5	10.5	6.7	17.1	9.6
With GCC links	8.1	11.0	6.2	5.0	6.5	6.4
Djibouti	—	0.0	—	3.6	—	2.9
Jordan	8.0	16.5	5.9	5.9	6.4	8.7
Lebanon	8.2	3.0	6.5	4.3	6.6	4.0
With EU links	35.6	16.3	11.7	7.2	19.6	10.4
Egypt, Arab Rep.	24.1	9.3	2.7	5.3	6.9	6.6
Agriculture Trade with World (SITC 0+1+2-27-28+4)						
MENA region	3.2	3.0	16.8	13.4	9.4	7.7

(continued next page)

Table C.19 *(continued)*

	Exports		Imports		Total trade[a]	
	1998–2000	*2008–10*	*1998–2000*	*2008–10*	*1998–2000*	*2008–10*
Oil exporters						
GCC	1.0	0.8	14.8	10.0	6.6	4.4
Bahrain	0.7	4.7	10.5	8.8	5.1	7.6
Kuwait	0.4	0.3	16.0	17.9	6.1	4.6
Oman	4.6	2.9	20.9	11.9	11.0	6.7
Qatar	0.1	0.1	12.8	7.9	4.0	2.7
Saudi Arabia	0.9	0.6	17.7	13.1	6.7	4.4
United Arab Emirates	0.8	1.1	11.3	7.1	6.3	4.2
Developing oil exporters	2.9	4.4	16.0	18.9	8.3	11.4
Algeria	0.3	0.3	31.1	19.6	12.1	8.0
Iran, Islamic Rep.	4.7	6.5	21.0	17.6	11.2	10.9
Iraq	1.0	0.1	1.8	—	1.3	—
Libya	—	—	—	—	—	—
Syrian Arab Republic	11.5	27.0	19.8	16.7	15.2	20.9
Yemen, Rep.	—	5.8	—	28.2	—	19.1
Oil importers	17.2	15.6	20.9	16.8	19.8	16.4
With GCC links	18.4	14.3	22.0	17.2	21.4	16.5
Djibouti	—	0.4	—	30.0	—	24.2
Jordan	16.8	15.5	24.0	18.0	22.2	17.3
Lebanon	21.4	13.0	20.8	16.0	20.8	15.5
With EU links	17.0	15.8	20.6	16.6	19.4	16.3
Egypt, Arab Rep.	15.6	16.9	27.7	21.1	25.3	19.6
Morocco	23.0	20.8	17.2	13.7	19.5	16.0
Tunisia	10.4	9.1	11.9	11.5	11.3	10.4

Source: Table C.16.

Note: — = Data not available or negligible.

a. Data may not add up horizontally (exports + imports) and are an underestimate because of missing and partial information.

Table C.20 Major Container Ports in the Mediterranean and Gulf Region

World ranking in TEU handled	Port	Country	Container traffic, 2010 (000 TEU)	Max quayside depth (m)	Lead terminal operator
10	Dubai	United Arab Emirates	11,600	16	Dubai Port World
28	Valencia	Spain	4,207		(local)
32	Jeddah	Saudi Arabia	3,830		Dubai Port World
33	Salalah	Oman	3,485	18.5	APMoeller (Denmark)
34	Port Said	Egypt, Arab Rep.	3,475	12.8	APMoeller
41	Gioa Tauro	Italy	2,851	16	APMoeller
43	Algeciras	Spain	2,810		APMoeller
46	Bandar Abbas	Iran, Islamic Rep.	2,592	15	(local)
49	Ambarli (Istanbul)	Turkey	2,540		(local)
53	Marsaxlokk	Malta	2,370	13	CMA-CGM (France)
60	Tanger Med	Morocco	2,058	9	APMoeller, CMA-CGM
63	Barcelona	Spain	1,946		Hutchison Whampoa (Hong Kong SAR, China)
86	Haifa	Israel	1,264		(local)
91	Damietta	Egypt, Arab Rep.	1,096	14.5	(local)
95	Mersin	Turkey	1,024	13.5	PSA (Singapore)
101	Beirut	Lebanon	949	10.5	Consortium of local, UK & U.S. firms

Source: Containerisation International.

Table C.21 Railway Performance Statistics, 2005[a]

Country	Morocco	Algeria	Tunisia	Egypt, Arab Rep.	Syrian Arab Republic	Jordan	Saudi Arabia	Iran, Islamic Rep.
Route length (km)	1,907	3,572	1,909	5,150	1,888	293	1,020	7,131
Freight's share of all traffic[b]	66%	61%	61%	9%	79%	100%	75%	63%
Freight tons (million/yr)	32.9	8.3	10.8	10.1	5.9	2.9	2.6	30.3
Freight average lead (km)	180	177	194	388	306	353	458	631
Freight ton-km (billion/yr)	5.9	1.5	2.1	3.9	2.2	1.0	1.2	19.1
Freight revenue ($m)	177	43	76	28	111	12	80	680
Traffic units per staff	958	229	556	490	194	1,707	991	2,210
Traffic units per km	4.67	0.67	1.52	8.69	1.28	3.50	1.55	4.25
Traffic units per locomotive	31.0	12.6	18.1	42.6	9.3	29.6	19.8	36.7
Freight revenue per ton-km ($¢)	3.0	2.9	3.7	0.7	4.9	1.2	6.7	3.6
Freight revenue per TK (PPP$)	0.08	0.06	0.11	0.03	0.08	0.04	0.17	0.06
Operating ratio w/normalization	82	107	107	147	87	137	137	73

Source: World Bank Railways Database 2005.

a. 2003 for the Syrian Arab Republic; b. Freight ton-km as % of total traffic units, i.e., freight ton-km as % of total traffic units, i.e., freight ton-km + passenger-km.

Table C.22 MENA Power Sector Key Indicators

Country	Population (millions)	GDP (US$ billions)	Electricity generation capacity (MW)	Peak electricity demand (MW)	Capacity reserve margin (%)	Electrical energy sales (TWh)	Average electricity tariff (US cents/kWh)
ECI[a]							
Egypt, Arab Rep.	83.0	441.6	24,504	22,079	11	119.4	2.5
Iraq	26.1	105.8	8210	9950	−17	26.9	1.2
Jordan	5.9	31.2	2979	2482	20	12.8	7.1
Syria	21.2	94.2	8025	7873	2	29.7	5.0
Lebanon	4.1	47.9	2312	2499	−7	4.9	6.1
WBG	3.9	4.0	140	810	−83	3.9	14.1
Libya	6.3	102	6006	5759	4	21.1	3.3
GCC							
Kuwait	2.7	121.1	12,579	10,970	15	49.3	0.6
Saudi Arabia	25.4	589.5	49,138	45,661	8	211.1	3.3
Bahrain	0.8	21.9	3227	2633	23	11.0	2.6
Qatar	1.7	71.0	7881	5090	55	18.8	2.2
United Arab Emirates	4.5	226.1	25,252	18,111	39	83.0	9.0
Oman	2.8	56.6	4100	3594	14	11.4	3.6

(continued next page)

Table C.22 (continued)

Country	Population (millions)	GDP (US$ billions)	Electricity generation capacity (MW)	Peak electricity demand (MW)	Capacity reserve margin (%)	Electrical energy sales (TWh)	Average electricity tariff (US cents/kWh)
Maghreb							
Algeria	34	276	11,332	7718	47	35.7	4.7
Morocco	31.3	136.9	5596	4550	23	23.3	11.2
Tunisia	10.3	82.1	3580	2793	28	12.9	9.5
Others							
Iran, Islamic Rep.	73.9	838.7	49,400	34,900	42	204.0	1.9
Yemen, Rep.	22.9	26.4	1334	1125	19	4.7	6.8
Djibouti	0.8	1.0	130	63	106	0.3	25.7

Source: Unless provided directly by the LAS, average tariff from February 2009 World Bank report, *Tapping a Hidden Resource—Energy Efficiency on the Middle East and North Africa.*
Notes: Population and GDP data based on World Bank Statistics for 2009. GDP data is based on purchasing power parity; Data reflect 2010 values supplied by the League of Arab States (LAS); Reserve margin is based on installed capacity. It may actually be lower depending on generation and fuel availability; GDP = gross domestic product, kWh = kilowatt-hour, TWh = terawatt-hour, MW = megawatt.
a. Egypt, Arab Rep., Iraq, Jordan, Libya, Lebanon, Syrian Arab Republic, Turkey, and West Bank and Gaza.

Table C.23 Power Exchanges in ECI[a] and Maghreb

Interconnection	Max transfer capacity (MW)	Energy exchanged (GWh/Year)	Load factor (%)
Algeria-Tunisia	150	141	11
Tunisia-Algeria	150	122	9
Morocco-Algeria	400	613	17
Algeria-Morocco	400	662	19
Morocco-Spain	700	15	0.2
Spain-Morocco	700	4,227	69
Syria-Jordan	200	20	1
Jordan-Syria	350	69	2
Syria-Lebanon	50	144	33
Lebanon-Syria	160	419	30
Jordan-West Bank and Gaza	20	158	90
Egypt, Arab Rep.-West Bank and Gaza	17	134	90
Turkey-Syria	250	97	4
Libya-Egypt, Arab Rep.	180	152	10
Egypt, Arab Rep.-Libya	180	70	4
Jordan-Egypt, Arab Rep.	200	9	1
Egypt, Arab Rep.-Jordan	450	363	9
Egypt, Arab Rep.-Syria		140	
Syria-Egypt, Arab Rep.		5	
Egypt, Arab Rep.-Lebanon		527	

Sources: League of Arab States and various World Bank reports.

Note: Data for 2010 or most recent year available; MW = megawatt; GWh = gigawatt-hour.

a. Egypt, Arab Rep., Iraq, Jordan, Libya, Lebanon, Syrian Arab Republic, Turkey, and West Bank and Gaza.

Table C.24 Key Institutions and Governance Documents in MENA Countries

		Regulator	Electricity law	Transmission grid code	Distribution grid code	Sector structure/ reform	Regional electricity forums
Maghreb	Algeria	CREG	Yes	Yes	Yes	SB/UNB	AUE, AMU, IMME, EU, COMELEC
	Morocco	No	No (RES)	No	No	SB/Part UNB	
	Tunisia	No	Decree	No	No	VER	
ECI[a]	Egypt, Arab Rep.	ERA	Yes (RES)	No	No	VER	AUE, AERF, Steering, Planning & Operating Committees
	Iraq	No	No	No	No	VER	
	Jordan	ERC	Yes (EE&RES)	Yes	Yes	SB/UNB	
	Lebanon	No	Yes (PPP)	No	No	VER	
	West Bank and Gaza	PERC	Yes	No	No	SB/UNB	
	Syrian Arab Republic	No	Yes (EE&PPP)	No	No	VER	
	Libya	No	No	No	No	VER	
GCC	Bahrain	No	No	No	No	SB/Part UNB	AUE, AERF, GCC Ministerial Committee, ARC, GCCIA
	Kuwait	No	No	No	No	VER	
	Oman	AER	Yes	Yes	Yes	SB/UNB	
	Qatar	No	Yes	Yes	Yes	SB/UNB	
	Saudi Arabia	ECRA	Yes (RES-Future)	Yes	Yes	VER	
Others	Yemen, Rep.	No	No	No	No	VER	AUE
	Iran, Islamic Rep.	Yes	Yes	Yes	—	SB/UNB[b]	
	Djibouti	No	No	No	No	VER	

Note: SB = single buyer, UNB = unbundling exists, VER = vertically integrated, — = no information, RES = renewable energy source, EE = energy efficiency, PPP = private-public partnership.

a. Egypt, Iraq, Jordan, Lebanon, Libya, Syria, Turkey, and West Bank and Gaza.

b. The Islamic Republic of Iran has a mandatory power pool with buyers purchasing their power requirements at the average pool price.

Table C.25   Regional Benchmark of ICT Infrastructure Status

	Penetration (%)				Prices ($)		Quality
	Fixed telephony penetration	Fixed broadband penetration	Mobile telephone service penetration	Mobile broadband penetration (3G + LTE)	Residential fixed broadband prices, OECD basket, low usage[a], low speed[b]	Real business avg. fixed broadband speed (kbps)	International Internet bandwidth (bits per capita)
Algeria	8.44	2.18	103.32	0.00	31.76	750	4.75
Bahrain	28.75	24.50	190.44	66.40	56.67	1,875	2,068.63
Egypt, Arab Rep.	11.43	1.97	88.05	21.27	51.49	937	1,219.85
Iran, Islamic Rep.	35.31	0.74	109.34	0.00	—	576	150.09
Iraq	6.19	0.00	77.78	0.00	—	—	2.57
Jordan	8.38	5.28	126.68	8.55	59.51	1,272	1,822.32
Kuwait	20.71	1.76	179.24	49.30	—	1,715	947.37
Lebanon	19.31	7.37	72.61	0.00	69.80	379	224.92
Libya	19.51	1.16	167.62	8.18	51.02	—	51.47
Morocco	11.86	1.68	110.66	9.36	23.53	2,156	1,618.48
Oman	10.12	2.18	146.30	34.47	57.63	—	1,432.45
Qatar	22.76	11.90	221.59	51.53	77.41	1,889	1,973.36
Saudi Arabia	17.04	6.29	220.46	52.14	25.46	2,205	1,639.82
Syrian Arab Republic	19.77	0.38	56.47	1.29	90.05	1,359	274.48
Tunisia	12.49	4.84	124.73	0.77	38.24	1,297	2,697.42
United Arab Emirates	32.58	18.40	273.71	92.31	31.79	3,222	8,769.80
West Bank and Gaza	9.21	3.53	88.17	0.00	91.07	1,295	313.14
Yemen, Rep.	4.15	0.37	41.14	1.85	50.19	—	28.71
MENA	16.56	5.25	133.24	22.08	53.71	1,495	1,402
OECD					31.75		
Eastern Europe	25.93	14.82	124.82	24.11		4,206	6,758

Sources: Akamai (Average Speed Connection) (Q2, 2011); Population data from World Bank database 2008; Telegeography Q2 2011; Teligent, Strategy Analytics 2011; World Bank database, 2009 or previous available year (in italics).

Note: — = Data not available or negligible.

a. Low usage: 2GB and 10 hours a month, in 60 minutes sessions, b. Download speeds from 256 to 512 Kbps except Bahrain (640 Kbps), Qatar (1Mbps), and Oman (2Mbps).

Table C.26 Examples of Greenfield (License Acquisitions) Transactions in MENA

Year	Target	Buyer	Price paid, $US millions	Percent stake acquired
2004	Maroc Telecom	Vivendi	1,400	16
2005	Turk Telecom	Oger Telecom	6,550	55
2006	Umniah	Batelco	415	96
2006	Investcom	MTN	5,530	100
2006	Tunisie Telecom	TECOM	2,250	35
2006	MobiTel	MTC	1,300	61
2007	Wataniya	Qtel	3,720	51
1998	Morocco	Telefonica/Portugal Telecom	897	
2001	Algeria	Orascom	737	
2002	Tunisia	Orascom	454	
2003	Algeria	Wataniya	421	
2004	Saudi Arabia	Etisalat	3,200	
2006	Egypt, Arab Rep.	Etisalat	2,930	
2007	Saudi Arabia	Zain	6,110	
2007	Iraq	Qtel	3,750	
2007	West Bank and Gaza	Wataniya	354	
2008	Qatar	Vodafone	2,120	
2009	Tunisia	Orange	206	
2009	Bahrain	STC	231	

Sources: Booz Allen Hamilton, 2007; MIGA database.

Table C.27 Trade between MENA Countries and PTA Partners (Nonfuel, US$ Millions)

PTA	Entry into force	Average of 3 years (million $)				Change in volume		% change	
		Exports		Imports		Exports	Imports	Exports	Imports
		Prior to PTA	Post PTA	Prior to PTA	Post PTA				
Jordan-US	12/17/2001	103	703	401	424	600	23	584	6
Bahrain-US	8/1/2006	237	287	278	627	50	349	21	126
Morocco-US	1/1/2006	243	442	615	1434	199	819	82	133
Oman-US	1/1/2009	55	212	917	908	156	−9	282	−1
Tunisia-EU	3/1/1998	3933	4215	5531	5864	282	334	7.2	6.0
Morocco-EU	3/1/2000	4517	5397	5656	6337	880	681	19.5	12.0
Jordan-EU	5/1/2002	77	99	1341	1675	22	334	28.2	24.9
Egypt, Arab Rep.-EU	6/1/2004	933	1338	3605	4232	405	627	43.4	17.4
Algeria-EU	9/1/2005	375	669	9571	15432	294	5861	78.2	61.2
Lebanon-EU	4/1/2006	193	425	2950	3426	232	476	119.9	16.1

Table C.28 Share of Trade between MENA Countries and PTA Partners in Total Trade (Nonfuel, %)

| PTA | Entry into force | Average of 3 Years (%) | | | | Change (% points) | |
| | | Exports | | Imports | | | |
		Prior to PTA	Post PTA	Prior to PTA	Post PTA	Exports	Imports
Jordan-US	12/17/2001	6.6	26.3	10.8	8.2	19.8	−2.6
Bahrain-US	8/1/2006	11.6	10.0	6.5	7.9	−1.6	1.4
Morocco-US	1/1/2006	2.5	2.7	4.3	5.7	0.2	1.4
Oman-US	1/1/2009	2.0	4.5	5.6	5.4	2.5	−0.2
Tunisia-EU	3/1/1998	78.7	79.6	76.5	75.3	0.9	−1.2
Morocco-EU	3/1/2000	70.5	75.1	66.3	66.4	4.6	0.1
Jordan-EU	5/1/2002	5.5	3.8	35.9	32.7	−1.7	−3.2
Egypt, Arab Rep.-EU	6/1/2004	31.2	26.1	31.4	27.8	−5.1	−3.5
Algeria-EU	9/1/2005	63.1	57.4	55.9	53.1	−5.6	−2.8
Lebanon-EU	4/1/2006	11.3	14.7	47.8	31.7	3.4	−16.1

Figure C.1   EU FDI (Outflows) to Selected MENA Subregions and Countries

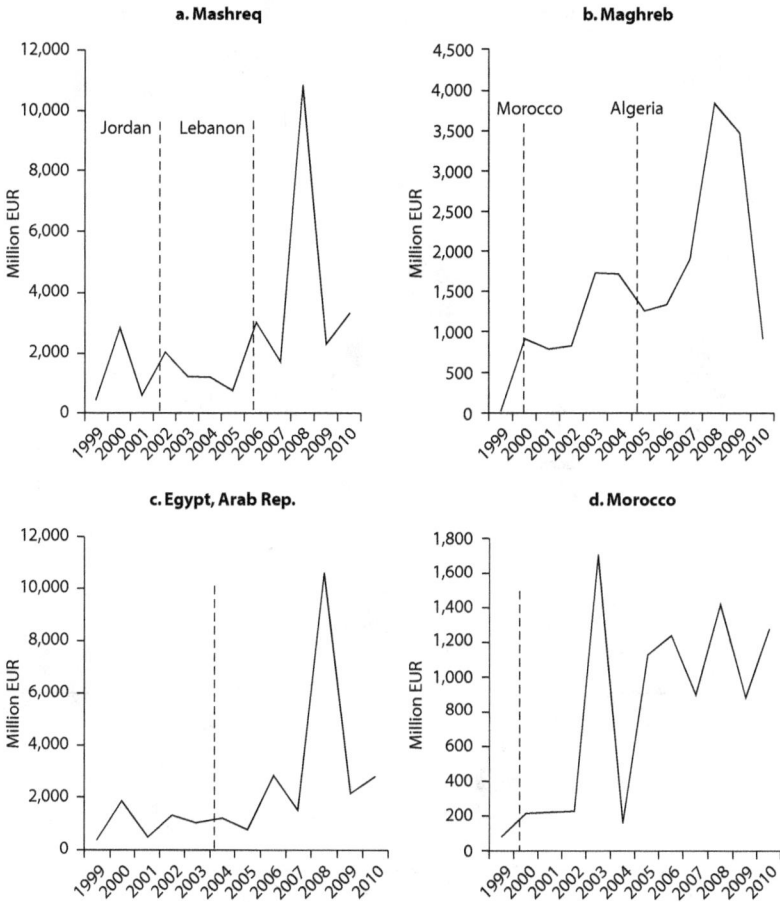

a. Mashreq

b. Maghreb

c. Egypt, Arab Rep.

d. Morocco

Source: EU direct investment outward flows by extra EU country of destination. EUROSTAT, Statistical Office of the European Communities, 2012.
Note: Dotted lines indicate the year of the signing of the Euromed Association Agreements.

Figure C.2   U.S. FDI (Outflows) to Selected MENA Countries

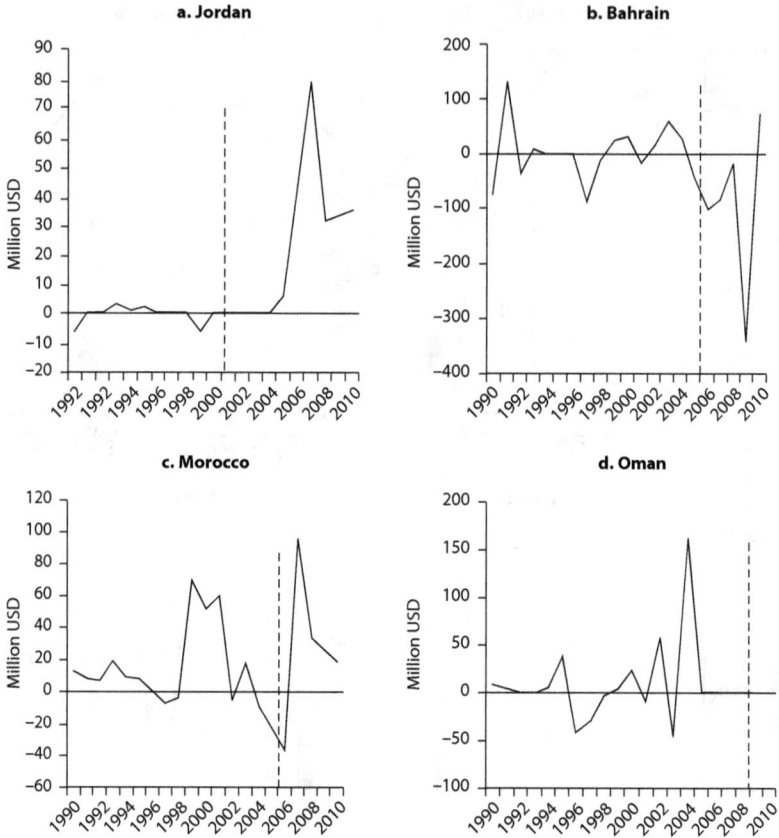

a. Jordan

b. Bahrain

c. Morocco

d. Oman

Source: U.S. Bureau of Economic Analysis, International Accounts, U.S. Direct Investment Abroad, Capital Outflows without Current-Cost Adjustment.
Note: Dotted lines indicate the year of the signing of the FTA with the United States.

Figure C.3   Euromed Association Agreements

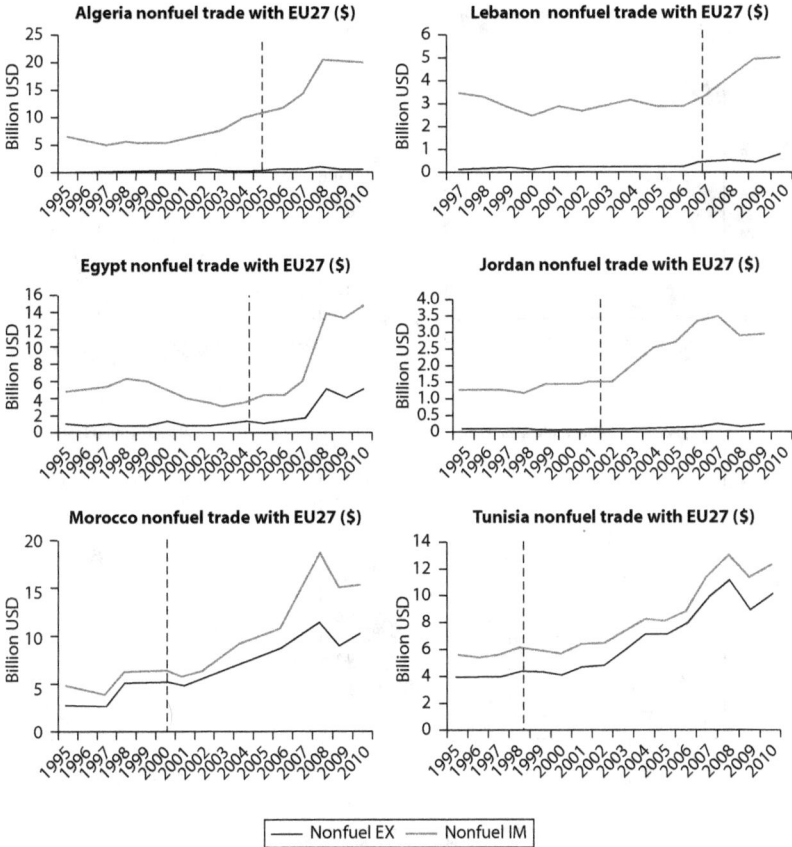

Algeria nonfuel trade with EU27 ($)

Lebanon nonfuel trade with EU27 ($)

Egypt nonfuel trade with EU27 ($)

Jordan nonfuel trade with EU27 ($)

Morocco nonfuel trade with EU27 ($)

Tunisia nonfuel trade with EU27 ($)

—— Nonfuel EX   ---- Nonfuel IM

Source: European Commission, Directorate-General for Trade, 2012.
Note: Dotted lines indicate the year of the signing of the Euromed Association Agreements.

Figure C.4   Free Trade Agreements with the United States

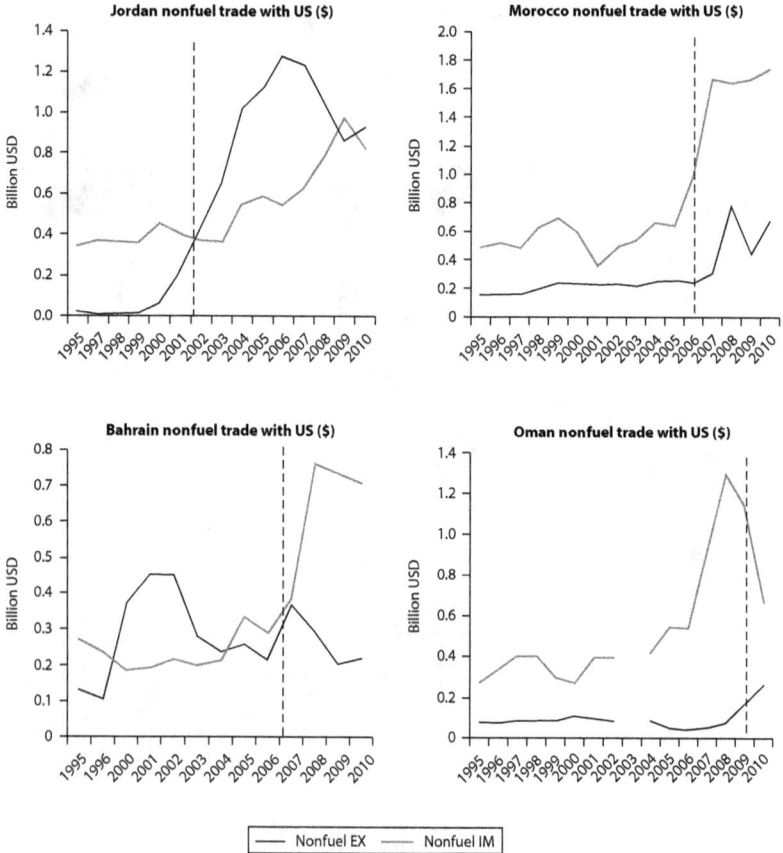

Source: Office of the United States Trade Representative (USTR), Executive Office of the President, 2012.
Note: Dotted lines indicate the year of the signing of the FTA with the United States.

www.ingramcontent.com/pod-product-compliance
Lightning Source LLC
Chambersburg PA
CBHW061734270326
41928CB00011B/2229